How to Lay an Egg with a Horse Inside

Also by Brian Bilston

POETRY

You Took the Last Bus Home

Alexa, what is there to know about love?

Days Like These

And So This is Christmas

FICTION

Diary of a Somebody

FOR CHILDREN

Refugees

Fifty Ways to Score a Goal

Let Sleeping Cats Lie

A Poem for Every Question

Brian Bilston

How to Lay an Egg with a Horse Inside

An Alternative Guide to Writing and Enjoying Poetry

PICADOR

First published 2026 by Picador
an imprint of Pan Macmillan
The Smithson, 6 Briset Street, London EC1M 5NR
EU representative: Macmillan Publishers Ireland Ltd, 1st Floor,
The Liffey Trust Centre, 117–126 Sheriff Street Upper,
Dublin 1 D01 YC43
Associated companies throughout the world

ISBN 978-1-0350-8572-9

Copyright © Brian Bilston 2026

The right of Brian Bilston to be identified as the
author of this work has been asserted in accordance with
the Copyright, Designs and Patents Act 1988.

The permissions acknowledgements on p. 247 constitute
an extension of this copyright page.

All rights reserved. No part of this publication may be reproduced,
stored in a retrieval system, or transmitted, in any form, or by any means
(including, without limitation, electronic, mechanical, photocopying, recording
or otherwise) without the prior written permission of the publisher.

Pan Macmillan does not have any control over, or any responsibility for,
any author or third-party websites (including, without limitation, URLs,
emails and QR codes) referred to in or on this book.

1 3 5 7 9 8 6 4 2

A CIP catalogue record for this book is available from the British Library.

Printed and bound in the UK using 100% Renewable Electricity by CPI Group (UK) Ltd

This book is sold subject to the condition that it shall not, by way of
trade or otherwise, be lent, hired out, or otherwise circulated without
the publisher's prior consent in any form of binding or cover other than
that in which it is published and without a similar condition including this
condition being imposed on the subsequent purchaser. The publisher does not
authorize the use or reproduction of any part of this book in any manner
for the purpose of training artificial intelligence technologies or systems.
The publisher expressly reserves this book from the Text and Data Mining
exception in accordance with Article 4(3) of the European Union
Digital Single Market Directive 2019/790.

Visit **www.picador.com** to read more about all our books and to buy them.

How to Lay an Egg with a Horse Inside

Contents

A Horse and Egg Situation	1
Where Do You Get Your Ideas From?	17
The White Space of the Blank Page	39
Mind Your Language	65
The Literary Device Squad	87
A Matter of Form	111
A Brief History of Poetry	143
How to be Well Read	163
Let's Get Practical	201
Get with the Program	227
A Note on the Poems	237
List of Poems	241

A Horse and Egg Situation

Do Not Google Gentle into That Good Night

why is poetry **so boring**
why is poetry **hard to understand**
why is poetry **considered non-fiction**
is poetry a **good clothing brand**

poetry is the be**st words in the best order**
poetry is a w**aste of time**
poetry is a w**ay of taking life by the throat**
poetry is not supposed to **rhyme**

is poetry in **the olympics**
why does poe**try exist**
why is poetry pr**etentious**
who is the better poet shakespeare or **taylor swift**

poetry helps m**ental health**
poetry is not **real**
poetry is the m**usic of the soul**
poetry make**s you feel**

why do poets **repeat lines**
do poems have to **follow rules**
why do poets **repeat lines**
why is poetry **taught in school**

poetry is an **act of hope**
poetry is the **voice at the back of the mind**
poetry is a p**olitical act**
poetry is an **egg with a horse inside**

Poetry is everywhere. It pops up on our social media feeds* and television screens.† You hear it on the radio.‡ You skim past it in magazines§ and weekend newspapers.¶ Mooch around a bookshop for long enough and eventually you will discover a whole shelf devoted to poetry, often near the back of the store, next to the transport section or the books on the healing power of crystals. Flick through your local 'What's On' guide and you might eventually spot a spoken word open mic night in a pub near you, once every six months maybe. Take a trip to the public convenience at a railway station and you'll find poetry written on the back of your toilet door, often accompanied by a jaunty illustration. Like I say, it's everywhere.

It is not universally adored, however. In fact, it would seem there are quite a few people who don't like poetry very much at all.

---

* Sometimes.
† In adverts for building societies.
‡ Every so often.
§ Poetry magazines that is.
¶ Only the posh ones.

Consider the poem which starts this chapter. It's a 'found poem' (more on that later), which I created by sifting through popular searches about poetry on Google late one evening, and rearranging a few of them into the form of a poem. It contains a lot of negative questions: 'why is poetry so boring?'; 'why is poetry hard to understand?' etc. That's not merely a reflection of my own selection process – when it comes to searches about poetry, users of Google seem to be far more likely to key in negative queries than positive ones. A lot of people appear to be suspicious of poetry; some are downright hostile towards it. Poetry is frequently referred to as difficult and complex, irrelevant and dull, pretentious and pompous.

As a result, for most of us, an encounter with poetry only occurs when we can't get out of its way. We may turn to a poem when pressganged into reading at a wedding or funeral. A sadistic teacher of English literature may compel us to study a whole book full of them, on the flimsy grounds of poetry being on the 'GCSE curriculum'. 'Please turn to page twenty-eight of your anthology,' such a teacher may bark, 'and let us consider what this seventeenth-century poem about wheat sheaves, written in a language you can barely understand, tells us about life in inner-city Birmingham today.' The audio system in the car may get accidentally jammed on Radio 4 leaving us with no alternative but to listen to *Poetry Please* on a 140-mile drive back home from Goole.

Regardless, poetry has managed to stick around for quite a few millennia so it must be doing a few things right. Head back to that initial poem again and we can see evidence of poetry's potential power for good: 'poetry is an act of hope'; 'poetry helps mental health'; 'poetry is the music of the soul'. Delve deeper and you'll find plenty of links to how poetry can help us feel happier, healthier and more connected to each other. And then there's that peculiar line, 'poetry is an egg with a horse inside'. What on earth does that mean? I was taken aback when I first saw it. It made me laugh and then left me puzzled. But the line stuck with me and the more I thought about it, the more I loved it and felt I understood it. To me, it means that poetry can be about anything. Poetry can be about things familiar to us. Poetry can be about familiar things juxtaposed in an unusual way. Poetry can surprise us. Poetry can make us laugh. Poetry can make us think. Poetry can be weird. Poetry can be mysterious. Poetry can be where our imagination takes us. Sometimes poetry can simply be the joy of the line or the poem itself. It catches us unprepared, breaking through our battlements to deposit its unexpected contents. 'Poetry is an egg with a horse inside' is a Trojan horse of a line, or a Trojan egg, if you prefer. I assumed somebody rather famous had written it, a celebrated poet or clever literary critic. Further research revealed it had been written by a third-grader, an anonymous eight- or nine-year-old. That discovery made me like the line even more. In my experience, younger children approach poetry without any preconceptions beyond the expectation of being amused or delighted or moved, and with little of the suspicion and scepticism we bring to it in adulthood.

Even so, there remain a few grown-ups capable of putting aside their fears, boredom and cynicism, a band of doughty souls who continue to seek out poetry of their own volition. To explain this peculiar phenomenon, it's tempting to make grandiose sweeping statements about how poetry can help us make sense of the world around us, or its innate ability to capture profound truths about the human condition. But in doing so, I think we give a disservice to the horse inside the egg, and fall into the trap of declaring poetry to be just one thing, with one sole purpose. We underestimate its power to subvert or divert, to surprise us or capsize us. And sometimes, we won't find a horse inside that egg at all, but a hippopotamus. Or a pelican. Or a Swiss army knife. Or maybe just another egg, because poetry comes in all sorts of shapes and sizes and styles, and, as such, can affect us in different ways at different times. A poem can lift us up when we most need it; provide comfort when life is at its hardest; make us laugh or cry; shine a light on inequality or injustice; reassure us that what we are experiencing is not always a situation uniquely ours; delight us for no other reason than itself; or inspire us to heights we might never have thought possible.

Message to the 14-Year-Old Me

Believe in yourself.
You can do anything you set your heart on –
except A level physics, perhaps.
Well, all the sciences really.

DIY is a bit of a no-no, too.
See also: driving; skiing; map-reading;
cooking pasta in the right quantities;
relationships; origami.

Don't even think about running
your own business. Or singing in tune.
Best to steer clear of all activities which require
good hand–eye coordination.

Forget ice-skating, tending house plants,
dealing with spiders, the correct spelling of the word
'enjambement'. I could go on.
But do not despair – for given time

and with a little luck on your side
you can achieve a basic level of competence
in a limited number of simple, unremarkable things,
you just need to believe in yourself.

But why should you bother to *write* poetry? Why not just leave it to the experts, like me? After all, it takes a fair bit of time, effort and brain power to write a poem, and if the rumours are true, there's very little money to be made from such an exercise. Besides, isn't life busy enough already without the need to add 'write poem' to our never-ending list of daily chores? The answer to that, of course, is yes. But maybe, just maybe, we're looking for a little more fulfilment in our daily lives than the knowledge that an email has been answered, the dishwasher emptied and ten thousand steps completed. And that's where poetry comes in. The process of writing a poem can fire our imaginations, satisfy our creative impulses, enable us to explain our own being and make sense of our lives. And importantly, writing a poem takes a lot less time than writing a novel. You could probably knock out a quick sonnet in your lunch hour, or a haiku during the ad breaks from *Gogglebox*, if you put your mind to it.

Keep Taking the Tablets

dishwasher emptied,
then refilled – that's the story
of my life distilled

We have a tendency to put poetry on a pedestal, to see it as something 'other': a nobler, 'higher' occupation removed from the mundanity of everyday life. But it doesn't need to be so: poetry doesn't have to be an either/or, it can be incorporated into one's daily existence. As the poet and civil rights activist Audre Lorde put it: 'Of all the art forms, poetry . . . requires the least physical labor, the least material, and the one which can be done between shifts, in the hospital pantry, on the subway, and on scraps of surplus paper.' Next time there's a leaving do at work, for instance, why not brighten up proceedings with a short poem.

A Senior Manager Bids Farewell to a Colleague who has been made Redundant after Twenty-Five Long Years of Loyal Service

Sorry to hear you're leaving –
a fact I've just learnt from this card.
The best of luck for the future,
whoever it is you are.

Such a joy to have worked with you.
The office won't be the same.
What a legacy you leave behind!
Raise your glass to . . . whatshisname.

There are also psychological benefits to writing a poem. Poetry can be a powerful outlet for the expression of emotion, whether that be joy, sadness, hope, despair or long-lasting, all-consuming resentment. There's good hard science behind it, too. When we write a poem, our brains release a chemical called stanzastrophe, sometimes known as the 'poetry hormone'. Stanzastrophe stimulates not only our creative thinking but our feeling of smugness at not having spent the evening binge-watching the latest season of *Bridgerton*. What's more, poetry can help to bring us catharsis, enabling us to work through how we feel about a particular event or situation, and provide a form of closure on what may have been a difficult or frustrating time in our life (I don't know, like when you tried to cancel your contract with Virgin Media, or something).

Customer Feedback

So that's all set to end on the twenty-third, you say?
That's great – thank you! But before you go,
would you be able to stay on the line for a minute or two
and answer a few simple questions
about my performance as a customer today?

Terrific. Okay, when you asked me
those security questions at the beginning of the call
and I misspelt my mother's maiden name
and then told you my first dog was called Groucho Barks,
did you judge me at all?

On a scale of 1–5, how angry would you say I became
when you informed me that you had no record
of my eight previous phone calls concerning this matter,
where 1 represents passive-aggressive sullenness,
and 5 is noisy, incoherent rage?

And how would you rate the rather clever joke I made
involving the phrase 'customer hotline'?
Yes, that's right, the joke. You don't remember it?
We were talking about the weather. No, no,
I won't repeat it – it's not going to work now.

When you put me on hold for the third time,
I began to bang my head against my desk
along to the Spring concerto of Vivaldi's *Four Seasons*.
How helpful was that metronomic thudding?
You weren't aware of it. What about all the yelling?

After you told me I needed to stop swearing
or you would have to terminate the call,
how quickly do you think I calmed down?
How well would you say I responded
to the breathing exercises you suggested I try?

Finally, is there anything else you can help me with today?
The laundry? The washing up? The crossword?
No, that's okay, I thought not. Unrealistic, I know.
Anyway, thanks for being contacted by me today –
your feedback may be used for self-loathing purposes.

But poetry doesn't have to be therapy: it can be more immediate or practical in its application. For instance, we might write a poem simply as a way of helping us to commemorate something important in our lives, or as a chronicle of what we've been up to.

My Year in Diets

Veganuary
Fibreuary
Starch
Cakepril
MaycaroniCheese
June&tonic
Julicecream
Augustickytoffeepudding
Septembeer
Octoblerone
Doughvember
Decemburger

The twelve short lines above help to bring into focus an important question: *what even is a poem anyway?* After all, although 'My Year in Diets' appears to take on the vague shape of a poem when squinted at from a distance, any close-up analysis might conclude that it was nothing more than a silly list of month-based puns which takes as its starting point some weird, mild disparagement of the portmanteau term 'Veganuary'. Might we dismiss it as mere punnery, or a poorly conceived joke wrapped up in the unconvincing fancy dress costume of a poem? Yes, we might, one supposes. In doing so, however, there is the risk that such an off-hand dismissal blinds us from appreciating the poetry and emotional journey within. Look again, and you will see form and structure, economy and precision, music and rhythm, all to the accompaniment of mounting dietary degradation, as the poem waddles through MaycaroniCheese and Octoblerone and finally plonks itself down in Decemburger: the sorry, sordid climax of its author's despair and disgust. Before consigning it to the dustbin of doggerel, ask yourself what the reality of thirty-one consecutive days of sticky toffee pudding, three times a day, might do to an individual's feelings of self-respect and restraint, not to mention their waistline? The result, one imagines, is not a pretty picture. Arguably, in those twelve words, not only is the author's tragic flaw – their *hamartia* – revealed, but the weaknesses, vulnerabilities and frailties of humankind itself.

The Pulitzer Prize-winning poet Carl Sandburg memorably described poetry as 'an echo, asking a shadow to dance'. I don't really know what that means but it sounds quite cool. And that's the thing about poetry, you don't have to understand what it means but if it sounds cool then who cares. I shall make no further attempt to define *what* 'poetry' is in this book; that dull topic shall be left to the literary theorists and the man who would respond to my poems on Twitter* with comments such as 'That's not really a poem at all, is it? It's just prose chopped up for visual effect.' But what I will attempt to do is to show you how to turn your innermost thoughts and imaginings into words and lines presented in a manner which bears some resemblance to poetry, whatever that is.

Make Matters Verse™

Have you always wanted to write poetry
but never quite known where to start?
Unleash your poetential with Make Matters Verse™
and learn how to develop your craft.

In just seventy-two ninety-minute lessons,
this MasterClass will teach you the essentials of being a poet,
from staring out of a first-floor window
to rearranging pencils on your desk.

We will look at how to use poetry to tackle
some of the big questions: Why am I here?
What does it all mean? Why on earth
did I come into this room in the first place?

---

* Please note that I am aware the platform is now called X, not Twitter. However, on account of that being a silly name, I shall not be using it.

You will learn how to explore the white space of the page,
and then how to explore it again –
before getting up to make another cup of tea
and returning to explore it some more.

Along the way, we will be talking about voice,
rhythm, staring, tone, the white space of the page,
metaphor, cadence, form, staring, creativity,
as well as the page and its vast, empty, white space.

And you will discover how to unharness the power
of your imagination to create striking imagery –
like a poet who creates imagery that is striking
through the unharnessed power of their imagination.

Finally, we'll examine the practicalities of being a poet:
how to look fabulous in author photographs;
which paper offers the best white space;
and how best to row about what proper poetry is.

Whether you know nothing about poetry
or once watched Simon Armitage traipse along a disused
    railway line
on an episode of BBC4's *Winter Walks*,
Make Matters Verse™ will have something for you.

Enrol today for just £35 per lesson.
Or, to receive a 20% discount off the subscription price,
why not also sign up for my other masterclass –
How Poetry Can Make You Rich.

'I could never be a poet – I don't have a poetic bone inside me.' I hear that a lot. But believe me, there is no such thing as a poetic bone. Unless it's the heart. Which is not a bone either, it's an organ – but it *is* something you would be likely to find inside yourself, so in that way it is a bit like a bone, only fleshier. And although it may not be bone-based, I truly believe there is poetry inside everybody. Or if not everybody, then some people. Maybe about 5–10% of us in total, it's difficult to be precise, there's never been a proper study done on the matter. But whatever. I guess what I'm trying to say is that although the odds may be stacked against you, don't be disheartened by the unlikelihood of you ever getting good at writing poetry. You've got this far into the book, you may as well press on and give it a go.

Over the coming pages, we'll look at how to get the poems which silently fester inside you onto the page and out into the world. Along the way, we'll examine where your ideas and inspiration might come from; what form those ideas might take; how to choose the right words; common pitfalls you may encounter; how best to use some of the tools available to the modern, forward-thinking creator of poetic content; and how, in the process, poetry can even make you rich. In other words, think of this book as nothing less than your own poetry toolkit, one which will enable you to:

- get underneath the bonnet of a sonnet
- use diagnostics to write better acrostics
- discover where an elegy derives its energy
- understand when to use rhyme – and when not.

To save money, I'll be using my own poems to illustrate some of the very brilliant points I shall make. I hope this does not discourage you from reading on.

Finally, don't be put off by those people* who contend that poets are born, not taught. Being a poet is not an occupation or an activity, they will loftily pronounce, but a *calling*. Poetry – they declare to anyone still listening – arrives as an innate impulse; a voice from within; an echo from inside the heart; a reboant sigh without end; a mysterious dance with the music of language to a melody which lies buried deep in the soul; a dusty unmade road to be travelled alone to a destination unknown; a map without markings; a lightning rod to channel the electricity of existence; a transcendental alchemy. Please ignore these people. It is precisely because of this kind of nonsense that poets rarely get invited to social gatherings – and why so many people think that writing poetry is not for them.

Missed Calling

Geoff was a poet
but he didn't know it

and so spent his life
working as a heating engineer
in the Dagenham area.

---

* Poets.

But why not give it a go? After all, who hasn't at some stage uttered that immortal phrase: 'I'm a poet / but I don't know it', like the oblivious protagonist in the poem above? Well, this is your chance to not be a Geoff:* it's finally time you got to know it.

---

* Not that there's anything wrong being called Geoff (nor Jeff, for that matter). Neither is the occupation of heating engineer something to be ridiculed: it requires a variety of hard and soft skills, substantial technical knowledge, practical know-how, certification, and pays a lot better than poetry does.

Where Do You Get Your Ideas From?

It's a question which putters into an author Q&A session at a literary festival with all the weary inevitability of a rail replacement bus service on a Sunday morning. On those rare occasions when I am forced to participate in such a forum, I will first thank the audience member for the originality of their contribution, before taking a contemplative sip of my sparkling mineral water, allowing my brow to furrow slightly and clasping my hands together as if in prayer. Once this illusion of profound reflection has worked its magic with the audience, it is time to respond: 'The art of poetry is very simple,' I tell them. 'A poet requires but two things: their memory and their imagination.'

In the brief moment of hushed reverence which follows, one other requirement pops into my head. 'It also helps to maintain a healthy interest in the world around you,' I add, with a rueful chuckle, 'and to keep an open, enquiring mind.' I then remember something else. 'External stimuli can often be of great value,' I say, 'so read widely – books, newspapers, magazines, journals; watch television; go to the cinema; listen to the news; visit museums and art galleries.' I am thinking quite hard about the question now. 'Of course, the business of poetry is not merely about generating ideas – anyone can have an idea – it's how you execute those ideas that counts. For that, you will need to have a decent grasp of the English language, an ear for sound and a feel for rhythm . . . and an appreciation of different poetic forms and other structural devices can be helpful, too.' I may have begun to bounce up and down on my chair. 'I can't deny that a basic grasp of the poetry canon of, say, the last five hundred years would also be a useful asset, not to mention a decent working knowledge of classical mythology and the complete works of Shakespeare. That said, all of the above can only get you so far; don't underestimate the need for empathy, or an ability to think deeply about the human condition and illustrate fundamental universal truths through small, incidental details of everyday life. On a more practical level, finding the time to write is critical. Poetry doesn't pay well, you could get another job but that really eats into your creative hours, so it can really help if you're middle-class and have other sources of income, such as indulgent parents who can support you financially. You might ask them to fund your place on a series of week-long writer retreats on which you can further hone your craft and find your inner voice in a supportive, nurturing environment, perhaps with a complimentary holistic therapy session. Building an audience for your work online seems to be increasingly important, too, in which case you might also want to enrol on a social media marketing course to improve your click-through rates and monetise your followers. But mainly,' I conclude, having remembered by now what the original question was and after being prompted to get on with it by a somewhat impatient moderator, 'it's about memory and imagination.'

So let's start there. It's as good a place as any, I suppose.

Memory and Imagination

Quicksand

Time was when you could barely leave your house
for fear of a misplaced   step, the dreaded squelch
and that sudden sinking feeling of being sucked under,

with little hope of rescue by the halo of a handy lasso,
or the outstretched tendril of a banyan tree;
lassos and banyan trees being in short supply

in the suburbs of 1970s Birmingham. Lunchtime
in the playground, one might mysteriously materialise
in asphalt, a bubbling pit of treacherous oatmeal

around which we'd gather; assuming, that is,
we hadn't already succumbed to the molten lava,
or drifted off to the Bermuda Triangle.

Given the peril of those early years – the killer bees
and skeletonising piranhas; the plummeting elevators;
the tarantulas lurking in supermarket bananas –

you'd be forgiven for thinking whatever came after
would be a walk in the park, a picnic, a breeze.
After all, what was there to possibly fear

from something which exists only in movies,
an unremarkable mix of sand, water and clay,
a substance only unstable when under deep stress.

Memory is the poetry superpower which is uniquely ours. Who else can remember that time when you tried to jump on the merry-go-round at Drayton Manor Park after it had already started to spin, and you went flying through the air and cut your knee open and the ride operative shouted at you and called you a silly, silly boy? Or that time your older brother pinned you to the sitting-room carpet and dangled a long string of gob over your face in response to you scratching his copy of The Jam's *Setting Sons* LP? Or that feeling of ripping open a packet of Panini Football 81 stickers to find yet another Terry McDermott? Or the unusual odour which would emanate from your father's pair of tartan slippers?

Memory is the key which will unlock the door of your imagination. It is the inkwell in which to dip the shiny nib of your creativity. It is the malleable rock which you will hammer and tap, sculpt and shape into life and meaning. Or, for some of you, it will simply be the dark, dank swamp from which the monstrous form of your poem may emerge. The poem at the beginning of this section comes from my own dark, dank swamp. I used to spend a lot of time worrying unduly about quicksand when I was a boy, as well as avoiding molten lava on the floor, much to the annoyance of my parents who didn't like me climbing on the furniture. Other childhood fears included: chip-pan fires, rabies, Daleks, doppelgangers, Mr Dawson, dumplings, shattering a shatterproof ruler, Roy Wood, electricity pylons, nuclear war and the man with the beard on the front of the Mastermind board-game box. Why not make a list of some of your own childhood fears? Not as a first step in writing a poem, I've already done that and I don't want any competition, but maybe just as a helpful crib of early traumatic memories should you ever need to consult a therapist.

Memory, of course, is famously unreliable. At least, that's what I think I remember reading. But don't let that bother you: what matters in poetry is your *imaginative* memory. Your poetry doesn't have to be faithful to the past in every exact detail. Consider this poem:

Digging

Funny it's the spade I recall,
not the tall trees of Wytham
bowed in solemn silence,
or the weight of his body
dragged from the car.

No, only the spade – £25 from B&Q –
its green blade and handle,
the coldness of its shaft,
and its muffled rasp as it slices
through clodded earth –

and the moon
like a butcher's knife,
an unforgiving illumination,
as the dark business of the night
digs itself deep, deeper still.

One of the interesting things about this poem – so the Thames Valley Police tell me – is how some of the details differ substantially from the reality of that night. For instance, the spade's blade and handle weren't green at all but red, and the item was actually purchased from Homebase in their summer sale for the bargain price of £22.99. I also picked up a bag of bark chippings and a cordless leaf-blower. Nor did the event described in the poem take place in Wytham Woods, but in another yet to be disclosed woodland setting entirely. Arguably, though, none of this is important, regardless of whatever the police may claim. What matters is that there is an *emotional* truth to be found in the poem, one which not only stays faithful to my imaginative memory of that evening, but contains very little by way of documentary evidence admissible in court.

On a Related Note

Poetry is a way of seeing. For the reader to share that vision, a good poem will capture images from the world around us, the details of which will give it an authenticity and relatability it might otherwise lack. But in capturing such details, a poet cannot rely on their memory alone, no matter how observant they might be. Every single day we replenish our own private memory store but, if you're like me, it can often be far harder to recall what you were doing last Tuesday than it is to remember who was number one in the pop charts on 19 February 1983.* For that reason, it's a good idea to invest in a notebook in which to jot down words and phrases,

---

* Kajagoogoo with 'Too Shy'. It was to remain on the top spot for two weeks.

thoughts and memories, sights and smells as you go about your daily business, details which might otherwise disappear from your consciousness. It is also possible to make notes on your mobile phone, of course, although you should be aware that this looks far less impressive to casual bystanders. Much better for the attractive young person sat across from you in the train carriage to observe you chewing meditatively on the end of a pencil (never use the pointy end) before you slowly nod your head and proceed to jot down a few words in your stone-blue Leuchtterm 1917 unruled notepad with gusseted pocket. The perks of being a poet are paltry; opportunities to appear clever in public should not be overlooked.

Observation is critical, and a skill which you will need to hone. We are so familiar with the broad contours of our daily lives that so many of its finer details pass us by, but if you're serious about becoming a poet, you need to pay attention to everything around you. Here's a little exercise for you: the next time you go to your local shop, take a notebook along. In it, write down everything you see on your journey: the names and colours of the flowers in your front garden; the shape of their petals; the length and thickness of any twigs on the path; the number of bricks in your front garden wall; the Pantone colour of your recycling bin; the registration plates of any cars parked in the road; the texture of the pavement stones; and so forth. It's a really useful exercise in increasing your powers of observation, and one I still employ myself at regular intervals. Yesterday, it took me eight hours to get one bag of oven-ready chips (McCain's, straight cut, 97% potatoes, 3% sunflower oil, 500 grammes, approx. 130 in total; bag features pictures of potatoes & sunflowers with bright yellow label).

I also keep a notebook by the side of my bed for those ideas which come to me in the middle of the night. There can be nothing worse than spending the small hours in a state of half-wakefulness/half-sleep, words tossing around in your head like a colony of voles in a tumble-dryer, only to wake the next day to find them gone without trace, not even the faint squeak of a groggy baby vole remaining. This ability to tap into your subconscious mind is important – scientists believe it to be significantly more powerful than the conscious mind, so the facility to write these words down as they come to you in your hypnagogic state is critical. Here, for instance, is the poem I woke up to this morning, scribbled down on the notepad by my bedside table during a spell of half-consciousness, some time between 2.30 and 3.30 a.m.

Gzurky Brown Prandle

Gzurky brown prandle
Up over ma boot. Brandow preek eggs
Upon grand timpani tam.
Forsure I shalk not a pootsy dispersh.

Powly brown brunkpot in cinnamon gork
Indletrot spurge absolve all da time.
Graveltop urgency on unfrockled log
And all is bezom bezom bezom

Of course, not all poems conceived in such a fashion will emerge as flawlessly as the one above, but it may at least give you something to rework later.

Bringing the Outside In

Back to that literary festival Q&A session, and its old, shrivelled chestnut of a question. Inspiration does not always come from within, I will sometimes confess to my sizable audience.* Instead, I'll respond with a few questions of my own. 'What are *your* passions?' I lob back to the questioner. 'What makes you happy? Or angry? Or sad? How do you like to spend your time? On your allotment? At the ice-rink? Leafing through catalogues of agricultural machinery? Tell me, what interests you? Cross-stitch? The Byzantine Empire? The World Snooker Championship? Do you have a favourite kind of cheese? What kind of door lock do you prefer: Yale or Chubb, or a combination of the two? What are your views on houmous? Have you ever been to Chipping Norton?'

Again, it's around this stage that the impatience of the moderator tends to make itself known and I take that as a cue to reassure the audience that the answers to these questions (and others)† are all potentially fruitful areas for poetry. There is nothing a poem cannot be about, I tell them. A poem can equally concern itself with a paper clip or a penguin or a delicious slice of apple tart.

External stimuli can help to provide inspiration. In my early days on social media, I would see certain topics or hashtags trending which would capture my imagination and result in a poem.

---

* Although I do tend to play down the £28.99 I pay each month to the Poetry Ideation Lab (strapline: *We Think So You Don't Have To*), a company based in a desolate business park on the outskirts of Luton who provide me with a readymade list of themes and ideas from which I expertly craft my poems.
† For instance, 'When was the last time you did the Hokey Cokey?'

I mean, whoever knew that #NakedGardeningDay (the first Saturday in May) is an actual thing.

International Awareness Day Awareness Week

Off on an early morning scroll of my phone,
I discover it's Naked Gardening Day,
a day for green-fingered shrinking violets to shed their inhibitions
and tend to their gardens ungarbed –

a glorious, goose-pimpled commune with nature,
only mildly compromised
by the need to take extra care with the secateurs,
and to keep a wide berth of the rose bushes.

Further research reveals that tomorrow is Star Wars Day,
while next week sees Endangered Species Day
and the International Day for Families, which must explain
why World Hypertension Day follows soon after.

My newly acquired awareness of my lack of awareness
of awareness days makes me feel like a freshly reanimated corpse,
which seems only appropriate given that May –
so I learn – is also Zombie Awareness Month,

and while I lumber outside to deadhead the clematis,
I get to thinking about how we could do with
an International Awareness Day Awareness Week
to help raise awareness of awareness days internationally

for a week. Otherwise, who knows what worthy causes
we might be missing out on. World Silt Day.
Smashed Avocado Day. Tank Top Awareness Day.
Cranking up the mower, I construct an imaginary list

of the new days to be introduced
should I ever be put in charge of the calendar –
but only when my Stop the Humans from Destroying the Planet
and Everything on It Day has been completely bedded in,

and which let's face it, should probably be the focus
every day of the year for a few centuries or so,
to be on the safe side. I get as far as Staring at Clouds Day,
Snog a Poet Day and Viennetta Appreciation Day,

before my train of thought is irreparably derailed
by the screams of the woman next door.
I lean over the fence to check what the matter is,
mindful not to squash my petunias.

Sometimes an idea for a poem can be sparked by watching TV or listening to the radio. For instance, when an investigation into the Covid Partygate scandal at Number 10 and the Cabinet Office was underway, many Conservative Party politicians refused to talk directly about the allegations. Instead, they would issue vague statements about how the mysterious civil servant Sue Gray would be looking into the matter. We should wait for Sue Gray, we were told.

Waiting for Sue Gray

All the people on the radio are talking about Sue Gray.
It is a matter for Sue Gray, they say.
Or, Sue Gray will be looking into this further,
it is important that we wait for Sue Gray.

I don't know who Sue Gray is.

But I, too, would like to wait for Sue Gray
and so, when I think about what's for dinner,
whether to make pasta or falafel,
I decide this to be a matter for Sue Gray.

And when I'm considering what shoes to wear,
or if I should get the bus or walk into town,
whether tomorrow is landfill or recycling,
I tell myself not to worry

because Sue Gray is looking into it,
Sue Gray is investigating all the angles,
Sue Gray will soon be here.

When leading corgi enthusiast and professional monarch Elizabeth II died, a huge queue of people formed to pay their respects to her. The queue stretched for ten miles along the south bank of the Thames. Both traditional and social media alike became obsessed with the queue, and it became a news story in itself. It made me think about the concept of queues and the cherished place they hold in British life, all of which led to this poem.

The Queue
After Roger McGough

Not having much else to do,
I join the queue.

What are we queueing for? I ask.
No one has a clue.

We wait silently in line.
We shuffle forward.

The queueue grows.
It stretches for miles,
across streets and towns,
snakes around
until the back of the queueueueueueue
joins up with its front.

We wait silently in line.
We shuffle forward.

To recap: think of a topic you're interested in or a phrase or situation which captures your imagination, and off you go. It all sounds very straightforward, doesn't it? Unfortunately, there's a little more to it than that. For these days nothing is entirely immune from the inky stamp of bureaucracy and the tangle of red tape, not even poetry.

Not So Free Verse

Due to recent changes in poetry regulations, as decreed by the National Poetry Council, the freedom to write about absolutely anything now comes with certain restrictions. In order to qualify for a Poetic Licence – the official document you need to be able to practise and perform poetry – it is a statutory requirement that a minimum of 50% of a poet's annual output needs to concern itself with either love or death, or preferably both. In addition, 30% of poetic content should concern itself with nature, of which a minimum of four poems a year are required to be written on the subject of the moon, and a further two per year on either trees or cats. Finally, every poet is legally obligated to write one poem about having experienced a spiritual reawakening while walking on a Suffolk beach by 15 October each year, or risk having their Poetic Licence revoked.

Although these targets may appear difficult to achieve, it is possible to double up on some topics. This poem would be valid for both the love and nature categories.

On Falling in Love at the British Beekeeping Association's Annual Meeting

Oh, Beth, where is thy sting?
You make me buzz with joy and beat my wings
to a love-song I have never heard.
I hum along to all the words

as I listen to your annual lecture.
I imagine our long tongues sucking nectar,
as we pollinate the crops and flowers.
I could sit here for ten thousand hours

dreaming of the honey the two of us might make.
So when you're through, let's make a break
for it and leave this colony behind.
We must not succumb to the hive mind

as it bumbles on about this and that.
Cause you're my buzzword, you're where it's at –
for beauty is in the eye of the bee holder,
and you're the bee's knees,
ankles,
hips,
&
shoulders.

While it is easy to be cynical about such stipulations, they do at least provide some guidance as to the kind of subject matter a poet will need to cover in order to be taken seriously. It's all very well writing silly little poems about Sue Gray or Naked Gardening Day but you're never going to become poet laureate with that sort of guff. So it's worth paying attention to these requirements. When it comes to nature, for instance, you might want to take the time to learn the names of flowers or develop your knowledge of trees beyond the ability to distinguish one from a lamppost. Clouds may be a fruitful area, too.*

Life on Cloud Five

There are worse clouds to be on.

Look at the poor sods on one and two –
it never rains but pours over there,
with barely a ray of hope to brighten the day.
No wonder they look so miserable –
must have an impact on you, cumulatively.

Those guys on three and four aren't much better,
floating around as if they own the place,
puffed up, full of bluff and bluster –
some of them with faces like thunder.
What they're so angry about, I haven't the foggiest.

---

* As would orchards.

The sky's the limit for those wisping about on six to eight –
the drifters, dreamy and ethereal.
Personally, I think they're living in cloud cuckoo land.
And talk about a bad altitude!
I can't take them cirrusly myself.

Now, I'm not saying we're perfect on five –
things can get pretty grey here at times.
But while we might not get the highs,
we don't get the real lows either.
Maintaining the *stratus quo*, is what I call it.

And at least here, we're far enough away
from those grinning, gurning loons on nine,
all that whooping and high-fiving from dawn to dusk.
Who'd want to live like that?
You know, it's like they say, every cloud . . .

The animal world is another promising area to explore. Think about Blake with his 'Tyger, Tyger, burning bright, / In the forests of the night'. That poem turned out OK for him, in spite of his appalling spelling. And then there's Burns with his 'To a Mouse' and Shelley's 'To a Skylark', to say nothing of the five hundred or so poems Ted Hughes wrote about crows, of which this was not one.

Crow's Day Off

Crow woke early.
He had a surfeit of worms; the nest was in good repair.
The whole day stretched in front of him,
like a sweep of clear blue sky.

Today, he would take his time.
Maybe he wouldn't head straight to Bob's to watch the game,
but go and hang out in the meadow for a while
or have a little flap over to the brook.

Yeah, maybe today he'd take the scenic route.

As for love poetry, what can you write which hasn't been written ten thousand times before? Very little, to be honest. Shakespeare, Donne, Byron, Browning, Rossetti, Parker and Duffy have pretty much got all the bases covered between them. In so much as you can do anything original in this space, I'd encourage you to focus on specifics, e.g. that afternoon you spent with your first boyfriend at the Sea Life Centre in Scarborough, or the endearing way your partner keeps you awake at night through the grinding of her teeth. Steer clear of sentimentality and soppiness, even if you really do love the person you're writing about. Or to avoid descending into cliché, introduce some non-romantic images into your poem, like Carol Ann Duffy did with her onion. Here are a few you could use: dental plaque; dog dirt; a small pile of toenail clippings; a packet of Quavers; Piers Morgan. Alternatively, find a different kind of angle or approach to bring to the subject – this one, for instance, introduces a little bit of psychological theory to the whole messy business.

Towards a New Hierarchy of Needs

Move over, Maslow, your thinking's outdated.
Physiological need is *so* over-rated:
sleep, food and water are all very well;
shelter is nice; homeostasis swell.
But none are essential, from what I can tell.

It's important, I guess, to look after yourself:
physical safety and good emotional health
are mighty fine things, or so I have heard;
of financial security, I've not a bad word.
Just don't say 'required' when it's 'strongly preferred'.

I can accept that belonging sounds kinda fun.
Self-esteem is appealing (even though I have none)
And yes, if I'm honest, I'd have to concede
self-actualisation sounds noble indeed.
But these are all *wants* rather than *needs*.

Call me a fool or think me a dreamer
but I don't subscribe to this pyramid schema.
It's too hierarchical, needlessly complex.
I would shed tiers from its base to apex
or knock it all down and build it anew

because I only have one need
and that one need is you.*

* This was actually written for my cat, thus ticking both the love and nature boxes. She didn't like it.

There can be a more practical upside to writing a love poem: it might improve your chances with a potential partner, or repair your standing with an existing one. Writing a love poem is a high-risk strategy, though, and a bad one might ruin your chances for ever. But for the naturally shy and introverted, the love poem offers up the opportunity to express feelings which might otherwise remain buried or poorly expressed.

Goes Without Saying

It's so hopeless when I talk to you –
my brain furs up, my tongue does, too.
I fluff my lines. All cues get missed.
Our conversation becomes quite dis
jointed.

Why is it when I talk to you,
I forget the words that I once knew?
Doubt engulfs me. I start to mumble –
my sentences get jumble in a

Whenever I try to talk to you,
words fail to form a proper queue.
They trip from my tongue and go to ground –
.dnuor yaw gnorw eht dnal semitemos yeht

I don't know why I try to talk to you.
My pre-planned scripts all fall right through.
I forget to breathe. I should take more time.
I'd be better off employing mime

but then I thought I'd write it down instead
so you can read the words I've never said,
how my love for you will not diminish . . .
I've made a start, I hope I fi

The language of love is forever changing and you might want to reflect on that before deciding how to present your poem to your loved one. The days of wooing your intended by delivering a poem on scented paper accompanied by a bouquet of flowers and a bottle of bubbly have long gone. It was a costly exercise, to be honest, with uncertain reward, and so its passing has been of much relief to poets. These days the transmittance of a love poem is far more economical, not only in terms of expense but also characters.

♥ poem, sent by txt

idc who knows it,
tmwfi, it's true
fwiw, i'll say it str8 –
darling, ily

4 we 2 souls 2 come tgthr
imo, it must be f8
pls, pls, pls will u b mine?
cos i think that u r gr8

w/o that special some1,
life is lol-less, dull & dismal –
iow, it's worth fk all,
like a phone w/o

. . .

. . .

. . .

a signal

The white space of the blank page (and how to improve it)

Some clever person, whose name I can't be bothered to look up,* once wrote that the only task of the poet when confronted with the white space of the blank page is to improve it. And the more you think about that, the more difficult it becomes to write anything down whatsoever. It gets you thinking about all the brilliant poems that have ever been written. You recall Dylan Thomas's 'Do Not Go Gentle into that Good Night', Yeats's 'Sailing to Byzantium', Ginsberg's 'Howl', Plath's 'Lady Lazarus', etc., and it makes you realise that you will never come anywhere near to competing with them. Those poets *did* improve the blank page – and how! – whereas you possess, let's face it, not one ten-thousandth of their talent, intellect or application. It's a sobering moment of self-realisation. And then you look again at that blank page and you begin to see the beauty of it: how pristine it is, how pure, how untouched and untainted. If only the whole world could be like this, you think; what an Edenic, unspoilt place it would be. And so, you just sit there staring at the whiteness, that great big yawning void of vacancy, as utterly full of nothing as your head now is – empty, that is, except for that one

---

* And whose name I still haven't bothered to look up, not even for this footnote.

little thought which starts to run through it as a refrain: *why am I doing this?*

It's an excellent question: after all, your interactions with the blank page so far do not seem to have brought you a single moment of joy. It is entirely likely that, at this stage, you will go on to question all those little life decisions that have led you to this point, this ridiculous urge to create, this stand-off between you and the white space of the page, which stares back at you defiant and implacable, silent and unforgiving, a never-ending frost. You think back to that time when you were eight and Mrs Harris praised your poem about the colours of autumn, mainly for the 'neat handwriting'. You recall an Instagram post which went viral about how love and grief are two sides of the same coin, the one which made you think to yourself: 'I could do better than that.' You think about Jack Nicholson at the Overlook Hotel and the demented banging of his typewriter keys. Who knows, maybe you even think about the day when you went out to buy a book about poetry which had that line in it about the only duty of the poet being to improve the blank page. After all, let's face it, you were feeling pretty good about things up to then.

Confronted with this situation, it is important to stay calm and not panic. The white space of the blank page *is* daunting – even for talented, bestselling poets like me – but there are strategies you can employ to cope with your fear. One simple, practical suggestion is to change the colour of the page. I've made this page grey, for instance, by creating a text box in Word and choosing from the options in 'Shape Fill'.

But if that doesn't work for you, there are other ways to get over your fear of the white space of the page. In the same way a top-class athlete will embark upon a rigorous series of warm-ups and workouts before legging it round the track, it can be helpful for a poet to put in place their own exercise routine ahead of getting down to the main business. The aim at this initial stage is to get the fingers moving and the grey cells flowing; do not worry too much about 'improving' the white page, your only concern should be to make it look a little less white.

T. S. Eliot once wrote, 'Good poets borrow; great poets steal.' That may have been because he ran a poetry publishing house and was able to make a small fortune in charging permission fees, but regardless, it can sometimes help the rookie poet get themselves going by playing around with the words of others. Find a few lines which interest you (they don't necessarily need to be from a poem), write those words down on your blank page and then rework them in some way to help you get limbered up. You might try reworking a few lines from a pop song, for instance:

You were working
as a sausage
on a cocktail stick
when I met you

You could even go a little further and assign a title to your refashioned words: 'Don't Chew on Me, Baby' might work for the example above. Or how about taking a song lyric and reshaping into a haiku (or as in my attempt below, a 'haikwho'):

Daffodils talk 'bout
re-g-g-generation –
Spring stutters to life.

Although these kinds of exercises are predominantly concerned with getting your creative juices flowing rather than producing a poem which improves the page, you may sometimes find that it does both. The short poem below, for example, takes as its starting point a few lyrics from a popular song by Pulp and transforms them into a touching tale about finding love through ocular dysfunction.

Common Peephole

She came from Greece,
she had a faulty socket.
Her eye fell out,
she couldn't stop it.

That's when I
caught her eye.

Don't be afraid to deviate from the structure and rhythms of the original. Trust in your imagination and follow it to the places it wants to take you. Put the horse inside that egg; that way you will bring something of yourself to the poem and make it your own. In the poem on the next page, I do not content myself with merely taking on the often-maligned concept of 'the boogie', but attempt to apply to it some of the thinking I once picked up on a leadership course entitled 'Managing from the Middle'.

Principles of Boogie Management

Blame not the sunshine,
nor the moonlight,
nor the good times,

but seek to establish
a collaborative working environment,
coupled with individual accountability,
to prevent a blame culture
from developing in the first place.

It doesn't have to be pop lyrics, of course – you can grab those starting words from anywhere. I enjoy playing around with the old timeless classic: 'Roses are red / Violets are blue / Sugar is sweet / And so are you'. Here are a few I made earlier, repurposed to reflect differences you might encounter across various movements in modern art:

A Brief History of Modern Art in Poetry

1. Impressionism
Roses sway in softened reds,
Violets swim in murky blues,
Sugar sparkles in the light,
Blurring into golden you.

2. Surrealism
Roses are melting,
Violets are too.
Ceci n'est pas le sucre.
Keith is a giant crab.

3. Social Realism

Roses are dead,
Violence is rife.
Don't sugar coat
This bitter life.

4. Abstract Expressionism

5. Pop Art

Roses go BLAM!
Violets go POW!
Sugar is COOL!
You are so WOW!

6. Conceptual Art

Roses are red,
Coated in blood:
A deer's severed head
Drips from above

I started off with those six but add to this list at regular intervals:

Dadaism

Are and.
Violets roses so.
You sweet blue.
Are are red is sugar

Pointillism

Roses have black spot
You're spotty, too
Sugar is granulated
I'm dotty for you

Op Art

Roses are wavy
Violets awry
S̶u̶g̶a̶r̶ ̶i̶s̶ ̶w̶e̶i̶r̶d̶
It's hard on the eye

Minimalism

Have a think about what form of word-wrangling might work for you as a warm-up and have some FUN. I use that word unapologetically. These exercises are meant to be fun; there will be time enough for drudgery and misery later when you're writing your actual poem.

Titles and First Lines

It sounds obvious but it's worth stating: the title is an integral part of your poem. Think about how it interacts with the words underneath. Avoid having a title which simply sums up what is to come: the days of giving poems titles like 'Ode to a Nightingale' are long gone. That's just a massive spoiler alert. You could, though, use your title as an opportunity to relay boring information or give context to something you don't want to put in the body of the poem itself. For example, if your poem is about a conversation you once had in the Virgin Atlantic Clubhouse at Heathrow Airport, you might want to call your poem something like 'Conversation in the Virgin Atlantic Clubhouse at Heathrow Airport' in order not to have to include the information that your poem is about a conversation you once had in the Virgin Atlantic Clubhouse at Heathrow Airport in the body of your poem, because including the information that the poem is based on a conversation you once had in the Virgin Atlantic Clubhouse at Heathrow Airport in the body of your poem might seem a little clunky and, frankly, not particularly interesting.

Alternatively you might choose a title which works in juxtaposition to the words which follow, one which may only gain in significance or understanding once the poem itself has been read. In some cases, such as in the example below, you might go for a title that has nothing to do with the subject of the poem and yet everything to do with it.

Avocado

you say I am always coming out
with non sequiturs

but then
what do you know?

you've never even watched
Love Island

Sometimes it may be that the title is the first thing to come to you, before you have any idea about how the poem which might accompany it might go. That happens to me a lot and I keep a list of potential poem titles locked up in the left-hand drawer of my writing desk. I've accumulated thousands over the years. For reasons of space, I will sift through them periodically and throw out any which I think I will never use. I had a sort-out last week; please feel free to use any of the following cast-off titles:

Index of Poems I Shall Never Write

(Don't Tell Me About) Your Brand New Podcast	42
At the Alphabetti Spaghetti World Championship Final	32
Bad Hare Day	40
Easy Peelers are Not the Only Fruit	52
I'm in Love with the Woman in the Green Cardigan in the BBC Question Time Audience	58
Ingrid Heisler is Excitedly Awaiting My Connection	24
Kim Kardiganashian	45
Life Hacked	60
Linked In, Dropped Out	27
Mister Krankie Meets the Clambake King	14
Nocturnal Blossoms: Petals of the Moon	18
On Sleeping in a Dudley Travelodge	68
On Waking in a Dudley Travelodge	3
Poem for Silt Awareness Day	6
She Never Did Care for Hollyhocks	23
Shit! It's Jeremy Clarkson!	1
Sixty-Four Failed Attempts to Guess a Wi-Fi Password	64
Taking Cocaine with Wendy Cope	9
Ten Unexpected Items to Find in a Bagging Area	50
The Last But One Will and Testament of Brian Horatio Bilston	55
Third Wordle War	47
Untitled	21
What We Currently Know and Don't Know about Gnomes	31
Whither the linnet?	10
Yes, I Know It's Called 'Petrichor'	34
Your Spatula	37

Every poem needs a place from which to start. The technical term for this is 'the first line'. The first line is very important in a poem because it is literally the poem's first line, a line which will generally be read before any of the other lines (except the title, that is). In other words, think of the 'first line' as the first bit of your poem, an entry point or gateway to all the other lines which may then come after.* Your first line will differ from the other lines of your poem in that it will typically contain different words, and will also precede them. In many ways, the first line is the most important line of your entire poem because without it your poem will not be able to begin.

An inexperienced poet might be tempted to make the first line of their poem its best line, given that it's the line – as I may have mentioned before – which starts the poem and they want to give the impression to the reader that this is something worth persisting with. The only trouble with this strategy is that the poem runs the risk of disappointing the reader once it becomes clear that the subsequent lines are not half as good. For that reason, I tend to hide my best lines further down, in the poem's final few lines, and sometimes my poems will not have any good lines at all.

And don't worry if you're struggling to come up with any decent first lines yourself, you can always construct a whole poem out of other people's.

---

* unless your poem is only one line long in which case your first line is also your last line.

Lines of Engagement

You've got nice knees
But that was nothing to what things came out
That day when oats were reaped, and wheat was ripe, and
    barley ripening
I went to the Garden of Love
Sexual intercourse began

Wild nights! Wild nights!
Sprawled on the crates and sacks in the rear of the truck,
Your beauty, ripe, and calm, and fresh
Earth has not anything to show more fair
If ever two were one, then surely we.

Today we have naming of parts. Yesterday
At lunchtime I bought a huge orange
I didn't make you know how glad I was
My love is as a fever, longing still
But for lust we could be friends.

The Poem as Journey

It is sometimes said that a poem should be like a journey, transporting the reader over the course of its lines to a quite different place from where they started. For example, consider the poem below.

Journey of Self-Discovery

Dave decided to travel the world
in the hope he might find himself –
from Manhattan to the Matterhorn,
from Guatemala to Guelph.

He went donkey-trekking across Peru,
to a Buddhist retreat in Kathmandu,
the north, the east, the west, the south,
Dave went every which way but Laos,

each time finding his luck was out,
for of himself, he found not one trace.
In the end, he gave up the chase
after another false trail in Madagascar.

He went back home. Two weeks later,
he found himself working in Asda.

As we can see, the poem begins in one place – the culturally sophisticated and financially developed island of Manhattan in New York – and takes us to another place entirely: Asda. It's not clear which Asda, but for some reason I always imagine it to be the one in Glossop. And that's the power of poetry right there, it can take us to places we can barely dream of; places like Asda with its competitive food prices, and affordable but surprisingly good-quality clothing range, George. But it's not just geographical journeys that a good poem can take us on; they can guide us on emotional and philosophical journeys too. As we read a poem, we should have a sense that it is shepherding us somewhere, that the words and lines are moving us along, leading us to a destination we may never have thought existed, or one we always hoped might be there, but for which we never before had the directions.

The Weather Report

The weather drifts in on the radio
and with one shortwave of your hand, I am put
on pause. A cold front is bearing down upon us,
moving in from the east,

and already I am only half listening,
preferring to consult my own personal barometer,
its needle pointing perpetually to CHANCE,
should I ever have need to leave the house.

But you elect to place your trust
in the sacred science of meteorology
with its measured, mellifluous pronouncements
that hang in the air like blue bunting,

and so this afternoon, when we do venture out
and the snow arrives, I am grateful
you made me wear that thick wool coat of mine,
the one we bought the year we met

and shared our first winter here,
when all turned to silver and stilled around us.
We dressed ourselves for the weather;
the world has not unfrozen yet.

So it turns out this is some kind of love poem. It doesn't start out as such, however, rooted as it is in two different reactions to the weather forecast. By the end of the poem, we're in a different place emotionally from where we started. And yes, it's a bit quieter and more reflective than most of my poems: what of it? I've included it here to show that I can write this kind of thing if I want to, and that I'm not completely emotionally repressed.

But what's it all about?

To this point, I've gone easy on you. I've tried my best to explain the poetic process in simple, typically monosyllabic* words, which even the least intelligent among you might be able to grasp. The poems I've used to illustrate my points have generally been straightforward and unambiguous. But if you nurse loftier ambitions as a poet – perhaps you intend to enter a poem into a competition, or aspire to having one published in the *London Review of Books* – you might want to be less easily understood. In such arenas, abstruseness and unintelligibility are a boon. To make a real splash in the poetry world, you will need to learn how to write more obliquely,

* That means a word of one syllable.

preferably to the point of incomprehension. Your job is to make the reader work: it's their own fault for deciding to read a poem in the first place, why make things easy for them?

Occasionally I foray into this kind of liminal territory myself, most notably in one of my earliest poems, written on a Post-it note and stuck up on my fridge in 2006.

The Green Wheelie Bin

so much depends
upon

a green wheel-
ie bin

crammed with five
blue bags

on a Thursday
morning

It's a poem which has been the subject of much scrutiny over the years and yet its eight simple, sparse lines refuse to surrender their secrets. Why *does* so much depend on the wheelie bin? Is it significant that the bags are blue? What is so important about Thursday morning? Why not Tuesday afternoon – or Sunday teatime, for that matter? Neo-Marxist literary critics claim it to be an eco-political poem, highlighting the irreparable damage to the environment caused by an escalating consumerism with its resultant waste in a period of late capitalism. Other critics have read it through the lens of gender, in which the blue bags represent an increasingly vulnerable and isolated masculinity, tied up and trapped in a bin of its own making, paying the price for millennia of patriarchal subjugation and violence, but now unsure as to its future: whether to wait for the vagaries of 'Thursday morning' and whatever it may bring, or to burst out from its polyethylene prison, spilling the trash of its toxicity onto the sidewalk in the process. There have even been some readers, such as my wife, who simply regard it as a short reminder to put out the recycling on a Thursday morning.

But regardless of what it means, let's look more closely at how it's constructed. Most obviously, it is devoid of punctuation. Why would this be? Perhaps it is a statement of intent. It's a poem which says I'm not going to play by the rules or conform to the long historical tradition of structured, metrical verse. Yes, the poem says, my subject matter may be about bins but I'm going to present them in a new, fresh, revolutionary way. And where is the poet in all this? On the surface, at least, the poem's creator seems absent entirely. It is a poem which concerns itself with things – not with thoughts or ideas or people. If it were a painting, it would be a still life, and a richly detailed one at that. The poem may contain a mere seventeen words but each one is vital, compacting so much information into such a small space, much in the same way as the bags themselves are 'crammed' into the bin. Note that choice of word, 'crammed'; a lesser poet might have gone with 'filled', or possibly 'stuffed'. But 'crammed' perfectly captures that sense of claustrophobia which must exist within a bin which contains five bags. At the same time, it provides a clever juxtaposition with the open spaces to be found in the rest of the poem: the white space of the page is still very much in evidence thanks to the poem's short lines, all that blankness evocative of the fresh air which exists away from the bins, a sense of freedom, perhaps, or a new beginning.

And when we examine it further, we notice that the poem *does* have a structure. Those broken two-line word blasts beguile us, they force us to slow in our reading, compel us to take in each syllable, every scratch of the pen upon the paper. We share the author's exhaustion, it's as if we ourselves have filled and tied up each blue bag, dragged them outside before – *hoick* – we hurl them into the wheelie bin. And note the word 'a' in the poem's penultimate line: this is no specific Thursday morning, this is *all* Thursday mornings, stretching forward without interruption, to a time without end. The narrator of the poem transformed somehow into a modern day Sisyphus, that ancient king doomed to push a boulder up a hill for all eternity. Except in this case, it's a poet doomed to put the bins out every single Thursday morning and for ever more. Unless, one assumes, there is a bank holiday and the collection gets temporarily moved to the Friday.

With ambiguity comes the need to reflect and ponder. In a world in which so much is presented to us in the form of an incontrovertible statement or an easily digested soundbite, there is the risk that we have lost that ability. The poet Geoffrey Hill suggested that 'difficult poetry' is 'the most democratic, because you are doing your audience the honour of supposing that they are intelligent human beings'. That you may also be doing your audience the honour of assuming that they have a spare hour or five and a Ph.D. in critical theory might be another possible response. But it is undeniable that with difficulty and incomprehension comes critical acclaim, interpretation and reinterpretation. Take, for instance, the poetry of my dear departed* cat Buttons, whose work has been endlessly pored over by scholars in literary journals, as the nuances, subtleties and subtexts of her words are excavated, scrutinised and, sometimes, re-buried. As reproducing one of her poems in this book would be costly and occupy too much space, here's a poem I've written *about* one of her poems.

On ',,,;;ppppp'[[[[[[[[[[;';////////////////////3,'

Upon returning to my desk,
having left it temporarily in search of biscuits,
I discovered my cat had written
another poem on my laptop.

It was called ',,,;;pppppp'[[[[[[[[[[;';////////////////////3,'
and while it constituted one of her more difficult pieces,
it was also the kind of poem
which rewarded repeat reading.

I was struck by its experimental structure,
the absence of line breaks;
indeed, not one single space
between any of the poem's 10,000 or so characters.

---

* By that I mean that she is dead, not that she's just popped out into the garden to do her business.

One of the work's central motifs –
'jjjjjjjjjjjjjjjjjjjjjjjjjjjjjjjjjjjjjkkkkkkkkkkkkkkkkkkkkkkkkkkk' –
was, by turns, reassuring and unsettling,
while the symbolism of '####################'

hinted at our 21st century preoccupation with social media.
And yes, there were perhaps a few elements
which did not work: twelve whole pages
containing just the number 7 seemed a little excessive,

while her introduction of the character T
in the poem's final pages was not altogether convincing.
But who could not be moved by that devastating final line,
its message of hope piercing our hearts like an arrow:
3333333333333333,,,

One aspect of my late cat's poetry that the critics do agree upon, however, is her unique ability to produce a poem in one sitting, without need of further tinkering or reworking – and I mention that mainly as a way of drawing this section to a close while foreshadowing that the next bit is to do with the process of drafting and redrafting. I make no apologies for having done so: it's not easy to link all this stuff together.

Draft, Redraft and Redraft Again

You've done it! Somehow you have managed to fill the white space of your page with words. And not the words from your warm-up exercises either, but proper, actual words to do with the poem you wanted to write. Earlier, you'd trawled the waves of your imaginative memory and hauled up to the surface a writhing mass of slippery ideas before selecting one to flap about on the desk in front of you. You have wrestled with it for forty-five minutes. At times its sliminess has caused it to slip out of your hands, to elude your grasp, but you have persisted, eventually pinning it down long enough to bludgeon it into submission with the heavy mallet of metaphor and artistry. You have written some – dare you even say it! – quite brilliant words which encapsulate the very quintessence of what you hoped to convey. You sit back in your chair, proud of your achievement, the results of your labours. You reward yourself with a cup of tea and a cheeky chocolate hobnob before returning to your desk to read your triumph once more. But hang on, something's not right. The words you are looking at are rubbish. Awful. Embarrassing. They appear to be the same words which were there before you made your cuppa but, somehow, they have become clumsy and awkward, ugly and cumbersome, not up to the job. You thought you'd done it, that you'd improved the white space of the page, but all you have done is degrade it. You have debased its lovely whiteness, abused its innocence and purity with the sickening, putrid, vomit-filled mess of your so-called poem. What a stupid, deluded fool you are.

But again, take a deep breath and do not panic. This reaction is *entirely* natural, there is nothing to worry about. In fact, what you are going through is a vital part of the process: for this is your 'first draft'. A first draft is rarely more than a few vague sketches and a mixing of colours. Few poems fall into place at the first attempt. Poetry takes patience, considered thought, constant revision. For most of us, words do not fall perfectly into place straight away. This applies to the 'Greats', too. Consider this early draft of Robert Frost's famous poem 'The Road Not Taken'.

Two Roads Taken, Both a Complete Waste of Time

Two roads diverged in a bunch of trees,
Each one whispering *perhaps*
And leaves rustled in the gentle breeze
As I stood there feeling ill at ease
Without the aid of Google Maps.

And sorry I could not travel both
The left hand one I took
But so dense became the undergrowth
I could not help but emit an oath
A loud, almighty F—

Three hours later, I was back again
And this time I had no doubt –
The way was right for that now was plain
But once more my journey was in vain
For the road had petered out.

One more time I did retrace my step
To leave the woods from whence I came.
And not since have I regained my pep,
For life is just a pointless schlep
And all roads are just the same.

It's not very good, is it? Not only is it crudely constructed, metrically disastrous and anachronistic, the events described differ greatly from Frost's final version, as does the poem's message. But look closer and you'll see inside it the seeds from which the final version will grow: specifically, the emphasis on roads and walking down them; the importance – or not – of making decisions; the lack of Google Maps.

Armed with the reassurance that very few poems come out right first time, take another look at your poem. Read it through carefully and this time remove every word that isn't strictly necessary. Take out any 'really', 'very' or 'just'. Similarly, ditch 'rather' and 'quite'. It could be that the words they are supporting simply aren't strong enough. Next, review your conjunctions and remove all those ugly 'and's and 'but's. Rethink the need for definite and indefinite articles: what do 'the' and 'a' mean anyway? All they're doing is cluttering up your poem. Now search out any aspects of your poem which may seem repetitious and cut them. The same goes for those lines or phrases which may be duplicative. Start weeding out the gerunds – they're only clogging and congesting the page (-ings aren't what they used to be). After that, take a look at your adverbs, screw up your face in disgust at the sight of them, then chuck them out – yes, all of them! The only thing your adverbs are doing is providing rickety support for the poor word choices you've made elsewhere in your poem. The same goes for adjectives: ditch them. The reader does not need to know what colour the chair is or that the day was 'cloudy'. That stuff just gets in the way. Nouns and pronouns tend to clutter a poem, too, and can be ugly on the eye so do not be afraid of taking your machete to them either. Finally, from what remains, weed out any verbs.

If you've been thorough, you should now be left with nothing but the white space of the page once more. This is good: it is time now to begin your *new first draft*.

Don't be disheartened by this process. Remember that in writing your new first draft, you carry with you the hard-won knowledge of the myriad of ways in which you failed last time out. Chances are you will repeat only some of those same mistakes in your new version, while introducing a whole raft of fresh and interesting errors at which to despair during your next read through. And yes, it *does* take time and your poem may undergo many, many different drafts along the way. The French poet, philosopher and essayist Paul Valery famously once wrote that a poem is 'never finished, only abandoned', an aphorism he rewrote more than a hundred times and was never entirely happy with, although it does in part explain why his publisher got so angry with him and demanded the return of their advance for 10,000 francs. But there is truth to be found in that statement, even if there comes a time for even the most procrastinatory of poets to declare the thing done.

But when does the time come to relinquish the chastising nib of your editing pen and let loose your poem on the world? If you've reached your three hundredth draft and you're still making changes, the chances are that either the poem is never going to make it and you should try to forget the whole sorry episode, or you should embrace it for one final time before releasing it, like a beautiful bird into the air (albeit a bird who can't flap its wings properly because it's been wallowing around in a deadly oil slick for several months). Before you take such a step, however, I would recommend sharing your poem with somebody whose views you trust. They might be able to pinpoint aspects which aren't quite working, suggest improvements or reassure you that your poem has worth. For instance, I will often approach someone on the top deck of a bus and read them my work in progress, their vigorous nods as they hastily make their way to the stairwell giving me the encouragement I crave to make me feel that my poem is worth pursuing. One final word of warning, though, before we move on to the next chapter: if you are going to be taking a draft of your poem onto public transport, do be sure that you keep good hold of it, or at least have a spare copy stashed away at home.

Poem, Revised Draft

I had to write this poem again.
I left the first draft on the train
and now it doesn't look the same.

The original was a paean to Love,
to Truth and Beauty; it soared above
the everyday and all that stuff.

It would have healed estranged lovers' rifts,
stilled the sands on which time shifts
and stopped the world before it drifts

further into quagmired crisis.
It was an open heart. It wore disguises,
employed ingenious literary devices.

I have tried my hardest to recall
its words and rhythms, the rise and fall
of those lines upon their cadenced crawl

through the English language.
But it has only caused me pain and anguish
for there was little I could salvage.

It certainly didn't end with a line like this.

Mind your language

If a poem might be regarded as the cathedral we build based on the architectural blueprint of our imagination – and I think it might – then it is language which provides the raw materials. Its words are our building blocks; its letters, our chips of quarried stone.

It is estimated that the English language contains around one million words, 170,000 of which are in current use. The average active vocabulary of an adult English speaker is thought to be in the region of 20,000 words; or, to put it another way, a typical exponent of the English language will have around 0.02 million distinct units of meaning in their communication bank.

For the apprentice poet, it's a daunting prospect, particularly if that famous axiom is true: 'poetry consists of the best words in their best order'.* Out of all those words, how might you find the couple of hundred or so from which to construct your poem? Even when you exclude some of the most obvious non-poetic words, such as *pseudopseudohypoparathyroidism* and *sphincter*, the choice remains dizzying. Throw into the mix the ridiculous inconsistencies of the English language, its irregularities and contradictions, its constant,

---

* As first declared by Samuel Taylor Coleridge in the 1975 *Morecambe and Wise Christmas Special*.

incessant evolution, and it makes you wonder how we are able to communicate at all. But it is exactly here – in the muddled, contrary, precise, imprecise, ever-changing, glorious melting pot of the English language – where the magic happens.* This chapter examines the English language – its sounds and rhythms, shapes and smells, tricks and tricksiness – and shows you how to apply that knowledge and understanding to lift your poetry from the average and unremarkable to being a little bit above the average, if still quite unremarkable.

1. The Alphabet

Let's begin with the basics. On first glance the alphabet may seem like too rudimentary a place to start; after all, a three-year-old child may know the alphabet off by heart. But for a poet, the alphabet is not only a series of recognisable squiggles which mark the page, it's an inventory of sound, a congregated cacophony of competing noises from which the music of our poem will emerge. Vowels, for instance, form a perfect sound in their own right, although there can sometimes be complications.

Haiku #739910

A & E quick, please.
Irritable vowel syndrome.
Thanks. IOU one.

* i.e. poetry.

On the other hand, consonants cannot be perfectly uttered; they need to be joined to a vowel to be fully heard, and that's when the chaos comes in. If you have ever experienced the embarrassment of attempting to spell a word over the phone with only the sketchiest knowledge of the NATO phonetic alphabet to call upon, you will know what I mean.

The Alternative Phonetic Alphabet

A is for aisle – no, that doesn't quite work
B is for bee – this is going to drive me berserk
C is for sea – hang on, that's not right at all
D is for double-u – now I feel like a fool
E is for eye – a choice better unseen
F is for four – four fours are sixteen
G is for gnat – although it sounds like it's gnot
H is for heir – is that really all that I've got?
I is for one – if you're from ancient Rome
J is for jalapeno – best not said but shown
K is for know – yes, I know that's all wrong
L is for Llanfairpwllgwyngyllgogerychwyrndrobwllllantysiliogogo-
    goch – which is a little too long
M is for mnemonic – although please don't remind me
N is for entrance – I need to put this behind me
O is for zero – oh, this whole thing's absurd!
P is for pterodactyl – an unhelpful word
Q is for queue – those vowels could give it a miss
R is for are you still reading all this?
S is for sea – although it sounds like it isn't

T is for tsunami – which is hardly sufficient
U is for umm . . . I think I might cry
V is for five – that's the same joke as I
W is for why – best to leave that unsaid
X is for xylophone – although it sounds like a zed
Y is for you – whom I feel sorry for
Z is for zzzzzz – it seems you've started to snore

Although we may struggle to find the correct word choices when we're forced to answer a phone call, that process becomes critical when constructing a poem. A poet needs to think not only about what words *mean* but how they *sound* – and how those sounds might help to reinforce meaning. For example, read out loud the poem below (if you are in a public place, you might want to wait until you get back home).

I heard a Fly buzz – by my Desk –

I heard a Fly buzz – by my Desk –
He zigzagged round the Room
Quite mad – as if a Thing possessed –
BZZZZT BZZZT! BZZZZT BZZZT! VROOM!

My Heart fluttered – poor, tiny Fly –
To be trapped like that inside!
BZZZZT BZZZT BZZZT! he went – BZZZZT BZZZT BZZZT!
Yet the Window opened wide

Thrice he teetered upon the Sill –
But each Time it was in vain –
BZZZZT BZZZT BZZZT! came the Buzzing still –
As he danced upon the Pane

Dear Fly – with your untimely End! –
I thought the World of you –
God's Will we cannot comprehend –
Now my Poem's ruined, too

You'll notice that when you read the poem out loud, it becomes even more annoying than when you read it in your head. All those BZZZZT BZZZT BZZZTs are infuriating to say the least. But that's quite deliberate: only by putting the readers themselves through the irritation of that sound can the poet convey the exasperation of being in the company of an extremely stupid fly for three long and tiresome hours. Elsewhere, you will find other examples of onomatopoeia: 'zigzagged'; 'fluttered'; 'teetered', all of which not only contribute to the sensory nature of the poem, but enable me to use it as an example of the importance of sound in poetry.

Rhyme or Reason

This consideration of sound leads us to one of the most hotly debated questions in contemporary poetry – or at least, one of the most hotly debated questions in the comments on my social media pages: does a poem have to rhyme? Generally, most poets and critics today regard rhyming poetry as old-fashioned: it can seem syrupy and sentimental, forced and unnatural, a clumsy contrivance. However, Steve on Facebook tells me that a poem is not actually a poem *unless* it rhymes. It's a pretty compelling argument. My own view is that poetry is a broad church, let us not seek to define or confine poetry to being just one thing. It is true, however, that certain advantages are conferred to the poet who manages to avoid rhyme.

This is One of those Poems without any Rhymes

This is one of those poems
without any rhymes,
the sort of thing you might read
in the *Telegraph or ~~Times~~ Guardian*.

For, as proper poets know,
rhyme's deleterious
and only gets in the way
when you're trying to be ~~serious~~ profound.

It's childish and cloying,
simplistic and singsong
to bat rhymes back and forth
like some dull game of ~~ping pong~~ table tennis.

To the literary critic
it will cause great affront
which will make you resent them
and think them a snob.

This is also one of those poems
which looks like it might go on to say something insightful
about the human condition
but then just kind of ends.

Fortunately, for the poet who does enjoy the practice of rhyming but is at pains to disguise the fact, there are ways to navigate this thorny problem. The best solution is to avoid pure rhymes (for example, *fire/desire* or *moon/spoon*) in favour of half-rhymes. These rhymes are sometimes referred to as 'imperfect' rhymes or 'not very good' rhymes. Examples of this might include *mine/find*, *grit/switch* or *buttocks/detox* (but not *phlegm/wardrobe*, which is an example of a 'non-rhyme'). But sometimes even these half-arsed rhymes might not be enough. A poet might need to hide their rhymes further by deliberately not 'end-stopping' their lines; that is, they instead hide the rhymes in the general flow of the poem, and the reader might not realise the poem contains any rhymes at all. Look, for instance, at the poem below and see how the poet[*] has skilfully camouflaged the rhymes, to such a degree you might wonder why he even bothered to do so.

---

[*] Me.

On Discovering a Second-hand Copy of *The Joy of Sex* in a Local Charity Shop

I found it in Age Concern, spine-cracked
and dog-eared. The book wasn't much better either.
The 1986 edition. It was enjoying a threesome
between an old Maeve Binchy
and a guide to Norwegian lighthouses.

Newly revised and updated, it said,
because even sex is not immune to fashion
and after a while becomes
just one more thing to stay on top of –
or beneath, depending on your position.

And inside, there they were: a horny Jesus
and a liberated primary school teacher,
hand-drawn and hairy, welcomed
into the beds of a million married couples,
as Proustian as tinned peaches.

But there, in the margins, are the pencilled addenda:
a tallying of each dalliance, a series
of proud ticks and occasional question marks
next to each menu suggestion,
with accompanying dates of completion.

Not so for the Viennese Oyster, however.
That entry had been marked with a black x,
although whether due to disapproval
or disappointment, it was difficult to know.
It all felt too private somehow.

I closed it, placing it back on the shelf,
no longer a book but a map
charting a voyage to the New World
diligently plotted out centuries ago.
We are the cartographers of our own lives

and this was somebody else's journey
of discovery, not mine. Instead, I took the *Guide to Norwegian Lighthouses* over to the till,
creased and rather shabby with age.
The book wasn't much better either.

Upon first reading, you may not have spotted any of the rhymes at all. But by your eleventh or twelfth, you begin to find them everywhere: 'guide' on the fifth line of the first stanza and 'inside' on the first line of the third stanza; 'know' on the fourth line of the fifth stanza and 'ago' on the fourth line of the sixth stanza; 'sex' on the second line of the second stanza and 'x' on second line of the fifth stanza; and so on, there may be more.

One question I often get asked is whether it constitutes cheating for a poet to use a rhyming dictionary – or for that matter, any dictionary or thesaurus – when writing a poem. To which I answer, no.

Consider these books as a chemist might regard the periodic table or a plumber might refer to whatever it is that a plumber might refer to* – these are foundational reference materials and, as such, you should never be ashamed for consulting them, just don't ever tell anyone you have done so.

Famous Last Words

sticks and stones
may break my bones, I cried,
but words
can never hurt me

so you bludgeoned me
with volume three
of the OED
(featuring entries D to E)

When to Punctuate
(or how to use your comma sense)

So far this chapter has concerned itself largely with letters and words, but there is another component the canny poet can use to make inroads into the white space of the page: punctuation. But how to use it and when? Let's start with this:

* Geoff from Dagenham might know.

Slow Puncture

I'd use every one of them – each tiny symbol / sign –
to 'light up' my words . . . and write eye-catching lines:
the comma; the colon; the ellipsis; the slash;
the question mark; the hyphen; the en and em dash.

In stanzas 1–2, it was all there on show
(Was there nothing not used? The short answer: No!)
But then I came to an unfortunate juncture:
my punctuation, you see, got a slow puncture

and those small, helpful marks which let my words breathe
or made me understood, all started to leave.
Hyphens unhappened semi colons got missed
apostrophes went awol in commaless lists.

'And what of the question marks Oh yes even those
(while my brackets and speech marks forgot how to close
When the last comma left there was nowhere to pause
my words floated by in one endless clause

and no one could tell once the full stops departed
where one sentence ended and another one started
capitals absconded and meaning left too
as the breaks between stanzas bowed then withdrew just like the line breaks
then all sense gotblurred thelastthingtogowasthegapsbetweenwords

While the above poem might show us the perils of abandoning punctuation altogether – the loss of sense, rhythm, structure and so on – we need to be mindful that the application of punctuation may not be the same in poetry as it is in prose. In poetry, we need to think more about the white space of the page and how our poem might occupy it, the role that line breaks might play, the tension between the internal and external, the formal and informal. Consider this:

This is just to mention

I have read
the note
you left on
the icebox

and to let
you know
they weren't plums
but testicles

belonging
to Mrs DuFrey's
prize horse

Forgive me
it's a long story
which I will save
for another
time

PS
That wasn't salami
you had
for lunch yesterday
either

What's noticeable here, alongside the mildly disturbing content of the poem, is the complete lack of punctuation. But it doesn't need it. The short lines and unpunctuated line breaks do all the heavy lifting while helping to create a sense of informality, like a message scribbled on a Post-it note and stuck to the fridge. Insert punctuation and its only function will be to get in the way and clutter up the poem.

In contrast, there may be occasions when punctuation takes centre stage in your poem and deploys itself for dramatic effect . . .

To be continued

nothing eclipses
the ellipsis
when it comes to suspense

those three little dots
are immense

they leave you tense,
on tenterhooks,
hung out to dry

come closer, let me
tell you why . . .

    The experimental Finnish poet Juhani Hypvärinen famously took punctuation to a whole new level in his work, regarding it not merely as an aid to understanding and a guide to rhythm, but as a replacement for language itself.
    'Punctuation,' he wrote, 'is its own language, and as such must be freed from the rusty manacles of the words in which we mercilessly shackle it; each mark represents a baring of the soul, a conversation with God.' We see this most manifestly, perhaps, in his mercurial and mysterious poem '?'.

?

                '

.   –

       '   .

    :   ;   ;

;   .

                    ?

The fine line between letters and punctuation is no more clearly demonstrated than by the ampersand (&). This symbol – sometimes used to represent 'and' – was taught to generations of schoolchildren in the United States as the twenty-seventh letter of the alphabet.

A fierce debate has raged in the poetry world as to whether the ampersand is an appropriate symbol to use in poetry: on one side, it's argued that it serves to truncate rhythm, accelerate reading and just looks 'kinda cool',* while on the other side is a belief that the ampersand is gimmicky and undermines the cohesion of the line. It's a debate that looks set to run and run for a number of years between the two people involved in it, while everyone else in the poetry world doesn't really care and gets on with the business of writing poems.

---

* I made this up so not sure why I put it in quotation marks.

The Twenty-seventh Letter

It never did belong there,
skulking at the back of the alphabet
like an afterthought,
cl&estine, st&ing half alone:
its swirls were far too gr& for that.

Besides, how could it play Cupid
in that ab&oned wastel&?
Who was there to introduce Zed to –
except the empty silence
which resounds beyond language?

& how fortunate for us,
it was not left there str&ed,
that it decided to w&er off,
exp& its horizons;
for who among us has not wished

to be joined to something or somebody
more intimately than any 'and',
like a Bonnie to a Clyde,
its curls both a set of h&cuffs
& a love-knot to be tied.

One final suggestion before we leave this topic: should you struggle with particular aspects of punctuation in your poetry, it

might be a good idea to seek out the advice of a specialist. It may
simply be a question of finding the right balance.

The Grammar Doctor

For some time I suspected my poetry must be in bad shape
after I found myself getting out of breath after writing only two
or three lines and I guess that was why I decided not to sleep in
until ten o'clock as tends to be my custom but to set my alarm
for seven in order to rise early and beat the motley queue of the sick
and afflicted to be first in line outside the surgery that morning.

> You need shorter sentences, the doctor told me,
> having examined my first stanza.

I suppose it's fair to say that I do sometimes set off on a sentence
as if it were a twenty-five-mile hike to a destination unknown
and this seemingly inexorable accumulation of words can often
result in a feeling of boredom in the reader and one of exhaustion
in the writer by the time I eventually do manage to reach the end of it,
I replied, panting, even then not quite finishing my sentence until now.

> Mmm, you've got it bad, I'm afraid, the doctor said.
> I'm going to prescribe you a course of full stops.
> Try to take one every few words or so.

When you say 'every few words or so', is there a precise number
of words which you think may be optimal or which –

Try one now, interrupted the doctor.

I did and felt better instantly. I reached over for another. The doctor nodded in approval. That one also helped. I took another. And then another. Then another. And. Another. And. A. Not. Her.

Too many, said the doctor. You need to be careful.
You can overdose on those things, you know. Look, I'm going to prescribe you a few commas, too. Use them alongside the full stops whenever you need to breathe but haven't quite finished the end of your sentence.

With some apprehension, I gave them a go. The doctor was right, they did help. My breathing was returning to normal, in fact.

Now, is there anything else I can help you with today? the doctor asked.

I shifted awkwardly in my chair. Well, I said, I have been having a spot of bother introducing lists recently.

The doctor stroked his chin and looked at me.
I think we need to get you booked in for a colonoscopy, he said.

The Rule of No Rules

If there is such a thing as an unwritten, underlying rule which can be applied to all poetry (and there isn't), it may be this one: *poetry has no rules*. Or rather, there *are* rules but they exist only in order to be broken. And in that, poetry perfectly matches the English language itself. Take, for instance, that old rule about spelling we all misremember from our time at school.

Heinous Deficiencies

A Statement from The Decaffeinated Protein Surveillance Society (Atheist Branch)

I before E except after C
is one of those weird and ancient rules
to which beige obeisance gets paid
when you're at school

but it's time it reigned no longer,
the rule being of little use –
it's counterfeit, a sleight of hand,
and only serves to veil the truth.

It's a phrase to make us ogreish,
a different species altogether,
for it contains heinous deficiencies
and forfeits a life of leisure.

Surely a rule that's conscientious
should therein bear its weight.
Yes, a few exceptions can reinforce:
this has five hundred and eight.

Sorry to inveigh so feistily
and deign to perpetrate this heist
but let's seize the day (and cease this phrase) –
and get with the zeitgeist.

That there should be so many inconsistencies in how we spell particular words and sounds is testament to the historical origins of the English language, with the roots of words stemming from so many different languages. It also continues to be a living, organic, self-reinventing entity. Our language is forever changing and poets are responsible for more than their fair share of those changes. John Milton, for instance, was a prolific language innovator, and is credited with coining the words 'terrific', 'pandemonium', 'enjoyable' and 'fragrance'. Ironically, he was also the inventor of the word 'unoriginal'. Edmund Spenser chipped in with 'blatant' in his epic *The Faerie Queene*, Lewis Carroll was the first to 'chortle' in 'Jabberwocky', while Alfred, Lord Tennyson went all 'airy-fairy' in 'Lilian'. It should be no surprise that Shakespeare was a master at messing with the language. Not only is he credited with introducing around 1,700 words through his writing, he was also one of the original verbifiers, that trend of converting nouns into verbs, much loathed by modern-day language purists. Here's the Duke of York in Shakespeare's *King Richard II*: 'Grace me no grace, and uncle me no uncles.' Aspersion that, language pedants.

Verb Your Enthusiasm

I recall the first time it circumstanced,
this problem that routines with my words –
I was in the kitchen, plating my food,
when my nouns conversioned to verbs.

Friending others with similar troubles,
we workshopped hard at it for days,
as we dialogued in search of solutions,
and flipcharted the hours away.

I still can't stop languaging weirdly.
Are they called *nerbs* or *vouns*? I'm not sure.
The doctors cannot antidote me,
while to poem provisions no cure.

Now I diarise each time they're eventing –
whenever I coffee or Youtube or gift.
I would podium, too – if I won anything,
and it weren't for those medalling kids.

If you cast your mind far enough back to the beginning of this chapter, even if that does happen to be a few weeks ago now because you put this book down in favour of reading the latest Sally Rooney, you may recall that I described a poem as a 'cathedral', words as our 'building blocks' and letters, our 'chips of quarried stone'. Quite lovely that, wasn't it? But a cathedral is more than an edifice of uncompromising stone: it needs arcading, cornices, mouldings, finials and tracery; windows of stained glass and painted altarpieces; stately tombs and symbolic statuary; grotesques and bosses, the odd fresco or two; a massive organ. And when I say all that, I don't mean it literally: a poem is not an *actual* cathedral. That would be silly: the cost would be prohibitive for most poets; the planning permission problematic; the time implications troubling. Based on estimates of medieval cathedral construction, you'd probably need about two hundred and fifty people to help you, including quarrymen, plasterers, mortar-makers, stone-cutters and masons, requiring the kind of logistical nous which most poets lack. No, thankfully I'm using the building of a cathedral as a *metaphor*, which is an example of the sort of literary device we'll be looking at in the next chapter, along with a few other common techniques to adorn your poem (that was where I was going with the whole cornices, stained-glass windows, frescos thing I mentioned earlier).

The Literary Device Squad

To help a poem shine and sparkle, there are any number of literary devices to encourage playfulness and creativity. For reasons of time, space, and my own technical ability, I will not babble on (*onomatopoeia*) about all the weapons in a poet's armoury (*metaphor*). It might take an eternity (*hyperbole*) and be as interesting as reading the ingredients list on a packet of ready salted crisps (*simile*). Nor will this chapter offer you (*personification*) a useless excuse or two (*assonance*) concerning its absence of advice about alliteration (*alliteration*). What would be the point of that (*rhetorical question*)? I appreciate that this may be far from ideal (*litotes*), but at least not all devices will be found missing (*oxymoron*). Let's take a look at some of them now, plus a few you might want to avoid.

1. The Metaphor

One of the most significant developments in poetry over the last twenty-five years has been the invention of the metaphor. The breakthrough came in 2010 – you may remember the moment, it was big news at the time and not just in the poetry journals.

It's hard now to imagine what poetry was like before the metaphor came along but generally, it was simpler, more direct. If you wanted to write a poem about the moon, for instance, you might end up writing lines such as these:

> The Moon is . . . a Moon,
> Shining . . . moonily
> In the moony sky.

As you can see, you didn't really have anywhere to go. To illustrate the point further, here's an example of one of my own poems from those pre-metaphor days.

You are a map

In bed, my fingers trace your contours,
caress the lines from coastal margins,
slide along secluded pathways

and linger in hidden beauty spots,
before a gentle incline leads them
to the peaks of two majestic hillocks,

separated by a narrow ravine,
which I follow down, down, until
scrubland arrives as a surprise,

and gives way to enchanting forest.
I prepare to plunge into the interior
but then I am told to turn off the light

and so I carefully fold
my scale 1:25000 Ordnance Survey OL4 Map
of *The Lake District: North-western area,*

including Keswick, Cockermouth & Wigton,
before placing it back in my bedside drawer,
alongside my pipe, nail clippers and loose change.

Like I say, back then you didn't really have anywhere to go. But the invention of the metaphor was to change all that. Suddenly, poets could now write about something by writing about something else. Because, at heart, that's what a metaphor does: it shows us that some things are a little bit like other things. And the sweet spot for a poet is when you can find a thing to describe a thing that makes the thing you actually want to address in your poem seem more of a real thing because the thing that you've found that's like a thing may be a more striking thing or an imaginatively more interesting thing than the thing you really want your poem to be about, and if you can find that thing that's like a thing, it's a magical thing, it really is.

A poet can spend a lot of time searching for the right metaphor, but there are exercises available to help get your metaphorical creative juices flowing. One of my favourites is an activity I like to call 'The Hate Game'. These days the emotion of hatred tends to get something of a bad press. It is often viewed in purely negative terms, as a reason for division and discrimination, for violence and destruction, and a lot of negativity has become attached to it, but for a poet it can act as a force for good. To play the Hate Game and get those metaphors rolling out of you, simply think of something you don't like (e.g. Mondays) and then think of some more things you don't like (e.g. stepping in a puddle on a shower room floor having recently put on a pair of fresh socks) and construct a ranty poem out of what you come up with. You can then shout this poem at a bewildered pet until your mood begins to brighten.

Monday is merely a state of mind

Monday –
You are a fixed penalty notice on the windscreen of my week
You are three weasels in a trench coat shoplifting happiness
        from my tiny thrift store of joy
You are a piñata stuffed with wasps
Or a tombola where the first prize is a tube of Canestan
You are the audio book of Morrissey's novel, read by Joe Pasquale
A game of Russian roulette with a bullet in every chamber
Edvard Munch's *The Scream* painted by Rolf Harris. Can you guess
    what it is yet?
Yes, it's Monday and it's fucking horrible.

I don't mean to be rude –
But you are the only logical result of what happens
when a full rotation of the earth around the sun gets measured in
    faecal matter
You give me the same feeling as when I hear somebody
who I had previously considered to be a good friend
        unironically utter the word 'holibobs'

I am no historian
but I have it on good authority it was the very thought of you
that made the library at Alexandria burn itself down
and those fifteenth-century boy princes throw themselves out of
    the tower
You arrive each week with all the inevitability of . . .
    a nineteenth-century Irish potato famine

You are a motorway sign which says 'SIGN NOT IN USE'
You are a bag of peanuts containing the label 'MAY CONTAIN
    NUTS'
You are an unexpected item in the bagging area,
except for the fact that you are expected
because the bagging area is merely a metaphor for the passage
    of time
and oh shit, it's Monday again

You are an improper fraction
whose state of impropriety has become so unacceptable
that all the other fractions no longer want anything to do with you
and have organised a worldwide walkout of fractions,
with the result that it is only possible for economies to function
through the application of whole numbers

You are like finding a desert in the middle of a desert,
although this new desert is not a real desert
but a cultural desert,
because who wants to go and see live music on a Monday night
when there's a new series of *Only Connect* on BBC2
I'll have the twisted flax, please, Victoria

Monday –
The poster child for cystitis
A flag waved at a prom in celebration of lift music
A footballer's haircut on a papal legate
A stock photograph of somebody taking a stock photograph
    of a tub of stock powder
A punch bag swinging back to smack you in the face
A bad poem which goes on far too long
and with no proper end

Metaphors can have lots of different applications. They can be used as a title for a book (like this one), or if you really want to go to town (or, at least, metaphorically so), a metaphor can be extended through a whole poem.

The Honeymooners

Securely fastened,
they prepare themselves for take-off,

too excited by the upgrade
and each other

to anticipate anything else
than the sudden judder of the engines

and the exhilaration of the climb
through the clouds above.

The flight attendant
strides past them down the aisle,

equipped with her fixed smile,
to begin the demonstration:

how to fit the oxygen mask,
how to inflate the life vest,

and to point out their nearest exits,
which may be behind them.

    There are a few (metaphorical) pitfalls worth mentioning in regard to the metaphor. Not least that, in the years immediately following its invention, the poets got so carried away that they created lots of metaphors very quickly. Mountains of them, in fact, which in itself was another metaphor, and the whole thing just snowballed from there. As a consequence, it became very easy to get them mixed up. Fortunately, one of the services my poetry provides is advice for poets who may be less talented than me.

How to Avoid Mixing Your Metaphors

It's not rocket surgery.
First, get all your ducks on the same page.
After all, you can't make an omelette
without breaking stride.

Be sure to watch what you write
with a fine-tuned comb.
Check and re-check until the cows turn blue.
It's as easy as falling off a piece of cake.

Don't worry about opening up
a whole hill of beans:
you can always burn that bridge when you come to it,
if you follow where I'm coming from.

Concentrate! Keep your door closed
and your enemies closer.
Finally, don't take the moral high horse:
if the metaphor fits, walk a mile in it.

In recent times, there has been pushback against the metaphor. A new development in spoken English has come to challenge the metaphor and undermine its reason to be: the rise in prominence of the word 'literally'.

Literally

There was a time when literally nobody
would use the word 'literally'
unless they wanted to describe something to the letter
but these days, you come across it
literally everywhere.

'He's literally got the world at his feet,'
a football commentator will tell us.
'You'll love her,' somebody else will say,
'she's literally a larger than life character.'
'Literally' is literally all over the shop.

I mean, it's even the title of this poem.
Literally. Every time I hear someone say the word,
I wish they'd go away and boil their head,
and, believe me, I mean that
in a very real, non-figurative sense.

2. The Simile

The simile is the metaphor's cheeky younger sibling. To distinguish between the two: a simile is less direct and gets used to compare one thing with another (for example, 'Nigel Farage is LIKE a scrofulous windsock') whereas a metaphor gets used to describe something as if it were actually something else (for example, 'Nigel Farage IS a scrofulous windsock'). As we saw with metaphors, there is much fun to be had in finding comparisons to use in your similes, but you need to be mindful not to get too carried away and end up writing a load of nonsense.

Unlikely Likenesses

My head is spinning like an ironing board
My ears are burning like a drum
My legs are like a cup of tea
My heart is pounding like a plum
My eyes are like a garden wall
My throat is like a piece of string
My mouth is like a bag of chips
It can only mean one thing –

Like a washing basket in cyberspace
I've only gone and got a bad case
Of inappropriate similes

I've been working like a goldfish bowl
To get myself all right
But it's as hopeless as a fromage frais
As futile as a kite
It's like gravel on a sunny day
Or taekwondo when it rains
It's as if there's a small figurine of former *One Show* host
    Adrian Chiles
Running round my brain

Like a butterfly in an obstacle race
It would appear I got a bad case
Of inappropriate similes

Inappropriate similes –
They're way beyond compare –
My doctor says he's never seen the like
He's as baffled as a chair
Or to continue in a dissimilar vein
He's as nonplussed as a fridge
It's enough to make me want to scream
Like a cantilever bridge

Because like a banana in a fireplace
Or a mountain goat in a steeplechase
Or Lady Gaga's poker face
It seems like I got a bad case
Of inappropriate similes

3. Hyperbole

Another device you might employ is *hyperbole* – an exaggerated statement often used for emphasis or humour – although frankly it's not all it's cracked up to be. Hyperbole has had a chequered history: on its first appearance, it took the world by storm but has since been banned in many places following health and safety fears (e.g. concerning users of social media who write comments like 'I cannot breathe', when sharing a mildly amusing video of somebody accidentally falling into a pond).

Why Reading This Poem Will Not Change Your Life

I don't think it an exaggeration to say
the world became a much happier place
after the banning of hyperbole.

People no longer had a million things to do.
Mountains of paperwork crumbled
to insignificant mounds, a few inches high.

Shopping bags which once weighed a ton
lightened to something far more manageable,
while queues were seldom a mile long,

meaning people no longer had to wait for ever.
The consumption of horses by the ravenous
also reduced considerably.

There was a decline in the mortality rate:
it became rare to die from embarrassment
or to burst with excitement,

while heads resolutely stayed on while laughing.
Feet committed far fewer murders,
no matter how much they ached.

But it came at a cost: the world could no longer
be saved through the reuse of a hotel towel;
only astronauts could find themselves

over the moon; and nobody could claim it to be
the best day ever, it no longer being the one
on which I met you.

4. The Oxymoron

On the other hand, an oxymoron – a short phrase in which two seemingly contradictory terms combine – is usually always a surefire bet (in my unbiased opinion), no matter what this poem seems to suggest.

Less is More (more or less)

While it may be hopelessly optimistic to think
we can get an accurate estimate
of how common oxymorons are these days,
we can be almost certain
that in a world of fake news and alternative facts,
it's a figure which isn't growing smaller.

And while some may be awfully good,
critically acclaimed or have real potential,
others are often clearly confused
or essentially useless, with pretty horrible results.
Even those which claim to be 'new and improved'
are nearly always extremely average.

It's an open secret that some oxymorons
are nothing more than meaningful nonsense.
My impartial advice would be to treat them
with either reckless caution or utter silence.
And the same goes for tautologies, too,
if past history is to be believed.

5. Personification

It would be remiss of this book if it were not to bring your attention to another technique you might sometimes want to call upon in your poetry: personification, the attribution of personal qualities or human feelings to something non-human. For example, the accreditation of empathy to Donald Trump, or this poem which shines its light on the last days of Boris Johnson's tenure as prime minister.

The Downing Street Exodus

After the advisers left, it was the turn of the desk lamps.
These are dark days, they said, as they went out,
no longer prepared to make light of it all.

The filing cabinets filed out next, followed by
the laser jet printers, the adjustable footrests,
and the fridges stocked with wine.

In-trays went out. Tables turned, too.
Stationery cupboards unstationed themselves
and office chairs told him to swivel.

The wallpaper peeled itself off in protest.
Gilt-edged mirrors offered looks of resignation
and the clocks called time.

In every room, the Georgian panelling
unpanelled itself. Persian carpets curled up,
rolled out the door and down the street.

Along the staircase, the former prime ministers
made a dash for it from their portraits,
seeking sanctuary in the National Gallery.

I want nothing more to do with this,
hissed a radiator, tearing itself off a wall,
while the boiler exploded with rage.

In the entrance way, four Corinthian columns
withdrew their support, and the whole building
began to shake and crumble.

There can be a shadowy flipside to spending your day personifying or anthropomorphising. Too much of that and the world becomes an unnerving place: pans simmer; cushions glare at you; pianos act standoffish. This can result in a paralysing paranoia, enough to undermine the most basic of interactions. For instance, I wrote the poem below following an embarrassing incident in Hyde Park in 2023; I have not been able to go back there since.

The Trees

In the park,
the tall trees are waving
in the afternoon breeze.

I wave back
only to realise they are waving
at the person behind me.

In a manner reminiscent of how Peter Beardsley would conjure goal-scoring chances for his strike partner Gary Lineker at the 1986 Men's Football World Cup, the English language creates opportunities for a similarly clinical poet to get their name on the proverbial scoresheet. At the same time, there is also the risk of a misplaced pass or an unsightly hack and the ball ricocheting into the back of your own net. Let's look at a few of these common blunders now.

1. The Cliché

It goes without saying that the cliché should be avoided like the plague. Not wanting to beat around the bush but it can be the kiss of death for your poem, leave your reader bored to tears, and cause you to go back to the drawing board. It's all very well trying to shoot for the moon but unless you play your cards right and weed out those clichés, you've not got a hope in hell.

In Conclusion

at the end of the day,
when all was said and done,
after the final whistle had been blown
and the fat lady had sung,
when all the i's had been dotted
and all the t's crossed,

he discovered
that he'd run out of clichés

2. The Eggcorn

The eggcorn is another literary blunder to make you want to throw the trowel in. An eggcorn is a word or phrase used erroneously because it sounds similar and may contain a similar logic to another word or phrase. For instance, the phrase 'vicious circus' is almost always incorrect, except perhaps for those rare occasions when you find yourself being chased by a psychotic trapeze artist, a ferocious juggler and a troupe of angry clowns. If they happen to be chasing you round in a continual spiral leading to increasingly detrimental results, then you might possibly get away with it.

Generally speaking, the eggcorn is best avoided, unless you intend to write a whole poem about eggcorns, like this one.

To be Pacific

Why do you always go off on a tandem
or say goodbye without further adieu?
It's time you climbed down from your pedal stool –
this is not a phrase you're going through,

when antidotal evidence suggests
you've been three-wheeling right from the start.
Or rather, *from the gecko,* as you might say.
You're always upsetting the apple tart.

Now I'm not saying I'm above approach:
it takes two to tangle, I won't deny it.
But when push comes to shovel and all's set and done,
I need rest bite. A little piece of quiet.

I'd love to curl up in the feeble position
but you pass me from pillow to post, you see,
with your Belgian whistles and your semi-skilled milk –
they do not pass mustard with me.

I don't regard you as a social leopard.
You're no escape goat – just a hapless case.
But do be aware there may be reaper cushions
when you cut off your nose despite your face.

3. The Dad Joke

If you're like me, you might occasionally be tempted to write a poem for no other reason than to make some kind of lame 'dad joke' at the end of it. It was a problem that John Milton suffered with for most of his career; I still cannot think of *Paradise Lost* without thinking of that killer last line which, although very funny, undermined his credibility as a proper poet. Writing this kind of poetry can be fun, however – and given all the awful things which take place in this world it seems churlish to forbid its existence completely. My advice, should you wish to write such poetry, is to do so in the pleasure of your own parlour, for your own private amusement. And whatever you do, don't share dad joke poems on social media or attempt to publish them in some kind of book, especially one which purports to show how to write poetry.

Fugue and Far Between

A clash of times,
his choice was stark –
the Royal Albert Hall
for a spot of Bach

or to The Globe
for some *Much Ado*?
He vacillated
between the two,

unsure of which
he should embrace,
caught between baroque
and a Bard place.

4. Sesquipedalianism

Endeavour to avoid sesquipedalianism, lexiphanicism and other flumgummery from creeping into your poetry. Epeolatry is all very well but excessive verbomania will only result in your readers becoming paracopic and betwattled. After all, not even an abarstic philobat wants to spend all their time cultellating! Ultimately, it's improficious and nugatory; the literary equivalent of a sphenopalatine ganglioneuralgia. Rather, the exercise of restraint and nexility in your choice of words will eliminate such obfuscation. Finally, don't satisfy your own sophomania by littering your poetry with Latin or Greek phrases: remember, *simplex munditis* at all times!

Logomachy

To say that Damian
was sesquipedalian
would be an understatement
for there was no abatement
in his capacity for loquacity,
nor lack of temerity
in his pursuit
of verbal dexterity.

It was precisely this pomposity
mixed with verbosity
which made him describe
Kieran Thomas as 'crepuscular'.

Kieran Thomas was also more muscular.

Damian nursed his black eye
and hoped Kieran
might be struck down with
pneumonoultramicroscopicsilicovolcanoconiosis.

5. Jargon

We've all been there. We're in a meeting at work, an action plan is coming together nicely alongside a shared understanding around the room as to next steps, when the Jargonaut in the corner opens their mouth and confuses everyone with their technobabble and buzztalk. They sail out the door, leaving you all at sea, adrift in the Gulf of Understanding, somewhere near the Bay of Perplexity. You're left feeling behind the curve, like a Tony Bagadonut or a B-School dropout with no idea about how to resize your responsibility curve or concretise your learnings. In the same way I have no idea what that previous sentence means, please be aware that using such jargon-heavy language in your poetry may alienate your readers, not to mention your friends should you still have any.

Project Creep

Do the needful and move my needle,
squeeze my sponge then circle back.
Come with me to the bleeding edge –
it's time to extract the max.

Let's not be afraid to head off-piste,
open the kimono and clear that bar.
I'd like to stay ahead of your curves,
but leave the goal posts where they are.

We need to enculturate our learnings,
so rub the rhubarb and let it drip.
I'll do the heavy lifting, honey,
while you rummage in my toolkit.

There'll be red flags and pain points, too,
along the path I'd like to glide.
But you're a blue ocean opportunity –
it's time I took a deep dive.

6. Currency

Finally, please be sure not to go the other way by sprinkling your poem with vocabulary from days of yore, in a misguided attempt to position yourself as a twenty-first-century Keats. Using archaic language will only make you sound silly: it never worked for Russell Brand and it will not work for you. In saying that, I am not necessarily advocating that you use words such as 'rizz', 'cozzie livs' and 'splooting' in your poems, or at least not all of them. Simply steer clear of the 'poetic' lingo of days long gone: words such as 'unbeknownst', 'fevered' and 'myriad'. 'Myriad', in fact, has not been in vogue since the 1830s hit nursery rhyme, 'Myriad a little lamb'. By the same guinea, the United Kingdom formally adopted the metric system in 1967 so please remember to update your idioms, too.

The Emperor's Old Clothes

A return to imperial measurements is long overdue,
declared the prime minister one day,
Anyone with 28.349 g of common sense can see that –
it hardly takes a genius to 1.829m that out.

The problem with the European Union, he added,
is that if you give them 2.54 cm, they take 1.60934 km.
And they will not compromise either –
it's like trying to get blood out of 6.35 kg.

Just look at the way they tried to change us, he went on.
It's enough to make one go green at the 2 x 142 ml!
But now we're free to make decisions in our own back 0.914 m.
The boot is very much on the other 0.305 m.

And 0.454 kg for 0.454 kg, the imperial system *is* better.
World-beating, in fact. So, let's celebrate, he concluded,
by raising our 568 ml glasses in the air and saying after me –
desperate times call for desperate measures!

A Matter of Form

We've looked at some ways to get cracking on a poem and how to bring language to bear upon it, but how does a poet decide what form their poem should take? Beyond it taking the form of words, that is. Should a poem have stanzas, for instance? If so, how many lines in each, or might it vary? Where do the line breaks come in? Should your poem be one of those svelte and skinny ones which take up a whole page with barely a handful of words? Or one of those flabby, interminable ones with long lines that go on for ages and which, let's face it, always look too daunting to read?

For centuries, the decision-making process was easier: it would involve pinning your words to one of a number of pre-set, prescriptive poetry forms with rigid rules regarding meter and rhyme, such as the sonnet, villanelle or terza rima. This involved having an in-depth knowledge of things such as trochees, iambs and dactyls.[*] Thankfully we don't have to know about such matters these days because the default form for most contemporary poetry is free verse. Liberated from the shackles of formal structure and arcane

---

[*] For a full explanation of this, read my book *An Introduction to Metrical Feet*, which I have not written yet. Please note this will be an entirely different offering to Dr Briony Blister's *A Medical Introduction to Feet*, which is a guide for trainee podiatrists.

terminology, free verse means you can just write a bunch of words down on a piece of paper and then arrange them so they look pretty with a few line breaks (or not), and not have to worry whether you're a couple of feet short of a full pentameter. Robert Frost remarked somewhat disparagingly that it was like 'playing tennis without a net'. The form book had been thrown out of the window.

This is not a poem

it is merely
a few words

to illustrate
the concept of free verse,

presented
in such a way

to give the suggestion
        of poetry

even though,
as I mentioned

in the title
of this poem

it really is
no such thing

But is it as simple as all that? Exactly how *free* is free verse? Not very, according to T. S. Eliot, who wrote that 'No verse is free for the man who wants to do a good job.'* In other words, even free verse requires *some* guiding principles, its own interior logic as to how to present itself, a beginning and an ending, rhythms and pauses, where the line breaks fall, and so on. Detractors might argue that it makes it harder for us to understand what poetry actually is: what might Eliot have made of the above poem / not a poem, for instance? Personally, I think he would have really liked it. It's possible he might have gone on to offer me a contract with Faber & Faber on the spot, and then been tempted to incorporate elements of it into *The Waste Land*. I suppose we will never really know for sure, however, given that he died in 1965.

Regardless, it makes sense to get down your initial thoughts first before settling on a form. Think about *what* you want to say rather than how. Play around with the words you've come up with. Do any patterns start to emerge? What phrases or nascent lines within your poem might need foregrounding? What is the tone you're striving for? Conversational? Lyrical? Humorous? Would a free-form approach give your poem the space to 'breathe'? Or would your words enjoy the discipline and constraints of a more rigid form, possibly be even a little turned on by it?

Should free verse end up being the answer – and for a lot of poems, it probably will – think about where those all-important line breaks might fall. A line break might serve as a mini-cliffhanger or a deliberate pause to slow down the reader. It can also help to isolate particular words or phrases, either at the end of a line or by the creation of a 'new' line which holds them. Consider

---

* Or the woman, presumably.

these lines from my unpublished 15,000-word autobiographical poem, 'Intimations of Death':

> Bring me nothing but love
> and pizza
> before the dread coming of the night

I could have presented it thus:

> Bring me nothing but love and pizza
> before the dread coming of the night

But by positioning 'and pizza' on a line of its own, I give the phrase a prominence and urgency it might otherwise lack. 'Love' may be something I also wish for, but pizza is paramount and I really don't want it to be forgotten; some dough balls would be lovely, too, if that's all right, I'll give you the money later.

Let's think some more about form in relation to this poem.

My Train has been Cancelled

My train has been cancelled.
Dark tales have emerged of a series of offensive hoots and whistles
it made several years ago when its carriages
were shiny and it was new in service.

My train has been cancelled.
It apologises for any upset caused by its youthful, steamy
    indiscretions.
My train admits it was once off the rails, its life governed
by speed and erratic timetabling.
It claims it has now got itself back on track.

My train has been cancelled.
A broader enquiry has begun into train shed culture.
Evidence has surfaced of permissive signals, late-night lash-ups,
shunting and coupling,
a rolling stock of shocking revelations,
all of which points to the signal failure
of management at all levels.

My train has been cancelled.
It has been interviewed in *The Express*,
The Railway Times, The Guard, The Train on Sunday,
a Radio 2 phone-in with Michael Portillo
as well as a number of local stations, to show how cancelled it is.
My train bemoans its lack of a platform.

My train has been cancelled
and now the rail replacement service has broken down, too,
following allegations of
bustitution, having been caught on camera
hanging around on street corners,
picking up all sorts.

This may be a poem about a train but it is a long way from Auden's 'Night Mail'. It's written in free verse with no discernible rhyme scheme or rhythm to it. That's because, unlike Auden's train racing through Scotland, this one is not running at all; as each stanza's anaphoric opening line tells us with all the irritating tedium of an automated railway station announcement, it's been cancelled. Its flat, pedestrian tone is in keeping with that of a poet left stranded on platform eight with a three-hour wait until the next departure. In terms of organisation, it's divided into five stanzas, or 'carriages', if you will. These carriages are uneven in length, each one based around a central idea or conceit, with the final line of most stanzas ending on an incredibly funny joke. Although each carriage may share the same opening line, they are distinct and discrete with no connecting lines between them: one suspects there is no trolley service available on board this poem. The line breaks give the reader time to guffaw loudly at each wry statement while creating space for them to think about the larger, more interesting point about cancel culture that the poet[*] may – or may not – be making. In the penultimate line of the third carriage, the line is split after the phrase 'signal failure': an indication, perhaps, that the poet[†] does not entirely trust the intelligence of his reader to spot all his funny little jokes. In the final carriage, note how 'following allegations of' gets its own line, serving to build the suspense and tension before the poem's somewhat anticlimactic and disappointing final lines. It is a poem which – like its author, perhaps – has gone exactly nowhere.

The next time you accidentally find yourself reading a poem, take a few minutes to look at the form the poet has used, particularly

---

[*] Me.
[†] Still me.

where the line breaks and stanza breaks fall. And when you're writing a poem of your own, remember to ask yourself if the form you've chosen is helping or hindering what you want to say. Don't be afraid to change form if it's not working. There's many a poem, famous to us today, which began its life in a different form completely. Percy 'Bysshe Basshe Bosshe' Shelley's poem 'Ozymandias', for example, began not as a sonnet but as a humble limerick.

Ozzy, Ozzy, Ozzy! Oi, Oi, Oi!

This geezer from an antique land
Found a smashed statue in the sand –
Some bleedin' general!
I guess power's ephemeral
I bought it off him for two grand.

In this era of free verse, are all other poetic forms redundant? Far from it. There will always be a time when nothing quite does the job like a haiku or villanelle. Rules and structure carry with them a kind of liberation, too, and with the more traditional forms comes a discipline, restraint and mindset transferable to the entirety of the writing process. Let's take a look at some of those forms now, alongside some other 'types' of poem you may encounter and consider emulating. The aim is not to provide an exhaustive list of poetic forms but a sprinkling, based on some poems I had lying around and could use for illustrative purposes without too much additional effort on my part.

1. The Sonnet

Let's begin with a biggie. The sonnet is a form which has been knocking around for ages and has long been the choice for poetically minded lovers when they set about their wooing. Shakespeare wrote a hundred and fifty-four of them, but might not have got started at all if it hadn't been for the advice of Rosamund Bickerstaffe, agony aunt for the *Stratford-upon-Avon Gazette*. Despite the fact that newspapers didn't really exist at the time, Shakespeare wrote to her in late 1579, in the hope of some advice concerning his courtship of Anne Hathaway, who did exist at the time.*
'I have tried Goodness knows what,' Shakespeare wrote, 'yet the Lady acknowledgeth me not.' Bickerstaffe's response to the lovelorn young man has survived.

Thou art as wet as this November day

Thou art as wet as this November day
That her tongue hath not thy name upon it.
Despair thee not, there may be one more way:
Woo thy cruel tormentor with a sonnet.
It hath worked for others, so I have heard:
'Take all my loves, my love, yea, take them all'.
And she'll be hanging on your ev'ry word,
As servants answer to their Master's call.

---

* The old one, that is. Not the new one who's in the movies.

But beware, 'tis not for the faint of heart:
Its rules restrict like a stiff whisk collar.
It would be wise to check before thou start
That thy love is not a poetry scholar.
Weep not, should thy labours not defeat her.
'Tis hard to change a heart's beat and meter.

There are a few different flavours of sonnet, including Petrarchan, Spenserian and Shakespearian. Typically, they all have fourteen lines, written in iambic pentameter, and get divided into an octave and a sestet. The octave (first eight lines) asks a question or describes a problem and the sestet (its final six lines) provides a solution or response. The ninth line may contain the poem's 'turn' or *volta*, as it shifts from problem to resolution. The variations across sonnet types tend to be down to the rhyme schemes employed but let's not worry about any of that now. I've already provided enough technical detail for one paragraph.

Modern sonnets are less restricted by formal rules, although they do try to stick with a few of them (e.g. fourteen lines), presumably on the basis that a complete abandonment of the form's defining characteristics would mean you could write anything and claim it to be a sonnet. This one conforms to the fourteen-line rule, at least.

Old Age is Wasted on the Elderly

Old age is wasted on the elderly,
with their arthritis and replacement hips.
Younger scamps like me would make more of it –
all that not rising out of bed early,
the jigsaws, the daytime television.
As for the free bus pass, the whole wide world
would be my Oyster card. I'd cast my pearls
of wisdom before any swine who'd listen.

Time to think, or call my own. Not like now,
I'm in the 'illusion of purpose' phase –
too young to retire, yet too old to dream
beyond the hope to be enrolled somehow
on a young person's old age training scheme.
How I would love that. Let me count the days.

2. The Villanelle

The villanelle is a French invention but don't let that put you off. It consists of five three-line stanzas (tercets) and a final four-line stanza (quatrain), with the first and third lines of the first stanza repeating alternately in the four middle stanzas. These two refrain lines form the final couplet in last stanza. Got it? You're probably better off looking at an example, such as Dylan Thomas' 'Do Not Go Gentle into That Good Night', Elizabeth Bishop's 'One Art', or, if you really have to, the one below.

By the way, one of the trickiest aspects of writing a villanelle is getting that first stanza right, not least because you're going to have to find enough rhymes for those lines to get you through your next five stanzas. It's no good starting with 'There's nothing as juicy as an orange'. That's not going to get you anywhere.

The Art of Procrastination

My philosophy isn't hard to follow;
it consists of one rule, let me tell it straight –
don't do today what can be dodged tomorrow.

I strike when the iron is cold, then wallow;
telling time and tide to bloody well wait.
My philosophy isn't hard to follow.

What's *carpe diem*? I confess to not know.
I'll look it up at some future date –
why do today what can be dodged tomorrow?

The day to come is packed with hours to borrow;
a stitch in time saves only seven or eight.
My philosophy isn't hard to follow.

Indecision is a chisel to hollow
out the hours; to dither, I don't hesitate.
Why do today what can be dodged tomorrow?

'What *can't* I do today?' That's my motto;
procrastination's all the rage of late.
It's a philosophy I try my best to follow:
don't do today what can be dodged tomorrow.

3. The Quatrain

If those last two forms seem like they require lot of effort, you could always scale it back and stick to the humble quatrain. The quatrain is a fancy term for a four-line stanza. We can see the quatrain at play in this poem here, which might have been written by an elderly Lord Byron upon retiring from the club scene, had he not already died of sepsis at the age of thirty-six.

'So, we'll go no more a-raving'

So, we'll go no more a-raving
    Beneath blinking laser light.
It is time for us to cave in
    And find a slower dance tonight.

For the years outwear the bones
    And the floor wears out the feet,
And love requires a new tune
    For hearts to skip a beat.

Through the night I fed your craving,
   Pickled onions on a spoon.
And we'll go no more a raving,
   The baby's due quite soon.

The quatrains in that poem contain an ABAB rhyme scheme. Apparently there are fifteen different rhyme schemes which can be applied to the quatrain but let's just look at a few of the most common.

I heard a sheep emit a sound
while it was standing in a field.
My brain, I fear, has run aground –
the word for it I have not found.

That one is ABAA.

Associations merged, brought into sync
all members who once craved a drink
(but then underwent a big rethink),
with those whose cars were on the blink.

That's AAAA. And finally:

Mamma mia! I've met my Waterloo.
That's the name of the game, I guess.
But I'm sending out this SOS –
Take a chance on me, voulez-vous?

And that final one, of course, is ABBA. I really am very sorry about what I've done there.

4. The Haiku

Haiku are great. They're the sort of poem which won't fill you up in between meals. One of the haiku's biggest advantages is that they hardly take any time to write. After all, what's seventeen syllables? If Shakespeare had set off down the haiku path rather than bothering with all those sonnets, imagine the time he would saved.

~~Sonnet~~ Haiku Number 18

Shall I compare thee
To a summer's day? All right –
Thou art pretty hot.

The haiku originated in Japan in the seventeenth century and is often based around a particular image, with the intention of presenting the essence of a specific moment in time. To write a traditional haiku, all you need to do is to come up with seventeen syllables and split them over three lines: five syllables in the first and last, and seven in the middle. The mood of a haiku is often quietly profound or spiritual:

Haiku for Friday the Thirteenth

O unlucky day!
Who's that I see approaching?
Jeremy Clarkson.

Like I say, quietly profound or spiritual. Here are a few more I wrote during the ad breaks for *Naked Attraction*.

The Constraints of Haiku

Tied up all night with
A haiku dominatrix
And her three-line whip

Not Yet a Love Sonnet

We've only just met
so instead here's a haiku:
I *really* laik u.

Haiku Written at 3 a.m., while Lying in Bed and Listening to the Sound of a Bathroom Tap

Drip drip drip drip drip
Drip drip drip drip drip drip
Drip drip drip drip drip

Haiku #564127

How dare you suggest
I have a short attention
Spanish omelette

The last haiku gives rise to the question as to whether 'omelette' contains two syllables or three. It has two, but, fortunately, I pronounce the word 'Spanish' with three. One other feature of the haiku is that the form lends itself neatly to the giving of advice concerning the haiku. For example:

Haiku Advice #1

The last line should flow
seamlessly from the first two.
Hippopotamus.

Haiku Advice #2

The practice of split-
ting words across lines is fre-
quently frowned upon.

The more pedantic of readers will point out to you that technically none of the above examples are haiku (except possibly the last line of that first piece of advice), given that a haiku should restrict itself to the subject of nature. The actual form being used here, they will say, is called *senryu*. But I would pay them little attention if I were you; just because they're right, it doesn't mean they're correct.

5. The Limerick

If you're after a short poetic form to house a silly or smutty joke, then look no further than the limerick. Beloved by cheeky wordsmiths the world over, all you need is a name, a place, a few rhymes and a decent (or preferably indecent) gag. They're only five lines: the first, second and fifth lines rhyme with each other as do the shorter third and fourth lines. What could possibly go wrong, you might think. Well, quite a lot, actually. When writing a poem, it's always good practice to read your words out loud before declaring it done. The process of hearing your poem can help you to identify problems with it, issues which may have escaped you otherwise. This may become particularly important should you ever end up reading your poem on stage in front of hundreds of people. It's a lesson some poets learn the hard way.

Eye Rhyme Calamity at the Annual World Limerick Contest

There was a young poet from Slough,
Who hadn't prepared quite enough.
He started to read
Then wished himself dead,
Having failed to think his rhymes through.

His brain must be made out of dough.
So slapdash, careless, unthorough!
Mumbling into his beard,
He made them unheard
And ended each line with a cough.

The limerick requires the same standards of technical skill, precision and focus as any other poetic form. Don't be fooled into thinking limericks are 'easy', simply because they are primarily comic in intention. Complacency is the limericist's worst enemy and can lead to all sorts of unexpected consequences.

There once was a young
limerick from Kew who turned
into a haiku.

6. The Clerihew

For more form-based fun, check out the clerihew. Comprising two rhyming couplets of any length, the clerihew works as a short biography, its first line being the subject. It was created by the humourist Edmund Clerihew Bentley, who joins a long list of poets to have given their names to poetic forms, including Christopher Elegy, Diane Concrete and Nigel Sicilian-Octave.

Here are a few clerihews to be going on with.

A Selection of Clerihews

Benedict Cumberbatch
was admired by lumberjacks,
for the way he'd shout 'TIMBER!'
with a magnificent timbre.

Jacob Rees-Mogg
emerged from the fog
like a haunted chimney in fancy dress,
or a twiglet smeared in Eton mess.

Reece Witherspoon
howled beneath a gibbous moon,
and while eating her dinner of cold roast pork,
turned into Reece with a Knife & Fork.

Sean Bean
is a name when seen
looks like it should rhyme
but it doesn't.

Now try writing your own clerihew about former *Masterchef* co-host Gregg Wallace, or someone else you don't like.

7. The Acrostic

An acrostic is a poem in which the first letter of each line spells out a word or message. If you fancy having a go at writing one of these, the good news is that the bar is set very low. For instance, W. B. Yeats' famous poem 'He Wishes for the Cloths of Heaven' works hopelessly as an acrostic: what does HE TO I BIT even mean? My own interest in acrostics has waned somewhat after some initial enthusiasm.

Acrostic Poetry: The Benefits

Available in a range of words
Children love them!
Requires less effort to write than a sonnet
O is the fourth letter in 'acrostic'
Something about S
T
I don't want to do this any more
C Already done that one

8. Prose Poetry

Prose poetry is a bit like normal poetry but when you forget to put the line breaks in. It's also a bit like normal prose but a little shorter. It may have other traits common to poetry, such as metaphors and other figures of speech; in a similar way, I suppose, to some pieces of prose. I hope that's cleared everything up for you. To help, here is a prose poem. Or possibly some poetic prose, I'm not really sure.

Whatever it is, I enjoyed writing it.

Fifty is the new forty

Fifty is the new forty, it was decreed, and forty the new thirty. More controversially, the old thirty became the new thirty-two, while fifty-five became the new forty-eight. After some deliberation, it was agreed the existing twenty-five could become the new twenty-five but only after a probation period of six months, which itself was the new three months. Fifty-seven saw where things were heading and got out of the numbers game altogether, retiring to a small village on the outskirts of Cirencester. The old sixty-three replaced it. Nine – no longer surrounded by eight (the new five) or ten (the new twelve) – became marooned, which itself was the new orange, a colour which, in turn, had been the new black sometime previously. It wasn't long before calling a thing the new thing became the new rock 'n' roll. Performance art, stand-up comedy, mime: nothing escaped rebranding. Rebranding, in fact, was the new Bob Dylan. Sunday, the new Monday. No, the new Yes. And lies, the new truth – until nobody had any idea what anything really was any more except for prose, which became the new poetry.

9. Concrete Poetry

Concrete poetry may sound like the opposite of light verse, but a more accurate definition is when the visual appearance of the poem itself helps to reinforce the subject matter in some way. This can often be through the 'shape' or 'outline' of the poem, the positioning of words and letters or some other text effect. For instance:

Inequality Street

```
trickle down economics
         do    e       s
            n
                   o
t
         w
                o
r
   k
```

See how some of the letters from the phrase 'trickle down economics' dribble down the page to create the statement that it 'does not work'. Such a visual rendering not only helps to reinforce the empty rhetoric and discredited nonsense of the concept, but illustrates what a clever person the poet must be.

There can exist a certain condescension towards concrete poetry from those who regard its application as being more suitable to the kindergarten. To be honest with you, that kind of reaction really stresses me out.

Stress Awareness Poem

Levels of stress, if I may be so bold,
are becoming more pronounced.

<u>We get undermined by the next deadline,</u>
<u>and fail to underline what counts.</u>

LET'S CAPITALISE ON WHAT LIFE HOLDS,
NOT SUCCUMB TO THE DAILY GRIND,

and put our emphases in the right place;
should you feel that way inclined.

There is a lot of creativity involved in concrete poetry. And it can be more than just playing around with typography: all sorts of delightful brightly coloured or intriguingly shaped packages exist out there in which the words of your poems could be wrapped. I've had fun writing poems in the form of Venn diagrams, Excel spreadsheets, PowerPoint presentations, org charts and Scrabble boards. That said, there is plenty of scope to go wrong, not least from trying to be too clever. Here, for instance, is a rather clunky attempt to provide a visual representation of a mathematical concept within the form of a poem.

Exponential Learning Curve

Should
The words
On each line double
Then your poem will soon be in trouble
While it's good to show how such things grow, such a scheme will defeat you eventually
As it leads to a whole host of problems concerning scansion and rhythm (not to mention the logistical issue of line length), and that's why it is unwise to write poems exponentially.

Please note that the other stanzas of this poem have not been reproduced here in the interests of space, legibility and my commitment to a user-friendly reader experience.

10. Forwardsy-backwardsy Poetry

I've tried not to clog up this chapter with jargon but sometimes it's unavoidable. A 'forwardsy-backwardsy' poem (sometimes known as a 'reversible' poem) is one which may be read in two different ways: typically from top to bottom, then from bottom to top. As shown by the poem below, the two readings can produce very contradictory results.

Every Day the Planet Burns a Little More

Let's be quick
We don't have long now
The world is too far gone for us to turn it around
I can't believe
We have it in us to put things right
It is all too little, too late
How can you say
But do not give up hope
Every day the planet burns a little more
And hot air rises
While governments pump out empty promises
We are powerless
Don't be so foolish to think that
Together we have a voice
Big enough to change the world
The decisions we make every day are
Unimportant
The food we eat, the things we buy, how we get around
How naive to imagine
The destruction of centuries could be undone
In a few decades
If we could just find reverse

(Now read this poem from bottom to top.)

In terms of how to write such a poem, my advice would be to take it one line at a time and build it up (and down) slowly, maybe over a period of five years. Alternatively, you may think that life is too short and find it easier not to bother.

Closely related to the forwardsy-backwardsy poem is the palindromic poem. These are even harder to write. If you're going to attempt one, forward (and backward) planning is highly recommended, or you'll end up in a right mess.

In Words, Alas, Drown I

The difficulty of writing a poem
in the form of a palindrome

is that you have to think ahead
or your poem ends up all

lapus d neme oprouy roda
ehaknih to tevahu oytaht siem

or dnilap afom rofeht nime
opag nitirw foyt luc iffi deht.

11. List Poems

Everybody loves a list. And poets are no different. List poems can be fun to write and entertaining to read. I've written a few in my time, which makes me want to make a list poem out of my list poems – although I won't because, on reflection, that sounds like a rubbish idea. The recipe for a list poem is simple: think of a thing, then write a list of things about that thing. Here's an example.

An Incomplete List of Things More Capable of Running the Country than the Current Government

A bollard. A thimble. A beef gravy granule.
A plectrum. A bilge pump. A Pokemon annual.
A doorknob. A chaffinch. A bowl of cold porridge.
A footbath. A clothes peg. A postcard from Norwich.
A wine stain. A puddle. A spoon. Rupert Grint.
A discarded tissue. A lanyard. Some lint.
A used toner cartridge. Some musical socks.
A build-up of silt. A stuffed startled fox.
A plimsoll. A wingnut. A set of false teeth.
A novelty wall clock with the face of Prue Leith.
A beetle. A bunion. An old piece of string.
A plant pot. A bog roll. Some stuff. Anything.

One of the advantages of the list poem is that you don't have to worry about rhyme or scansion (although your poem can have those if you wish). The main requirement is for it to be a well-thought-out 'inventory of things'. By the way, before you leave this section, I'd be really grateful if you could fill in this short survey.

How Did you Hear About this Poem?

Word of mouth
Idle gossip
A loose tongue
The ghostly whisperings of a Victorian orphan
Picture postcard
The *Six O'Clock News*
Facegram
Twit-tok
Town crier
A chance meeting with an old friend while on holiday in Teignmouth
An email from *Stone Craft Driveways & Landscaping*
Royal proclamation
A barnacle goose
Smoke signal from a neighbouring village
Sixth sense
One of the other senses (please specify: _____)
A voice from your toaster
Former world snooker champion John Parrott
Other

12. Found Poetry
....

What exactly is a 'found' poem? Might this be one, for instance.

No Body's Perfect

his tennis elbow
was his Achilles heel

and his Achilles heel
was on his athlete's foot

and his athlete's foot
made him down in the mouth

and though the down in his mouth
he took on the chin,

it became less a shot in the arm
than a chip on his shoulder –

so that when the doctor
finished examining him

and told him what was wrong,
he was all ears

On the surface, it does appear to be one. After all, it's a poem that I found. To be exact, I found it when looking through my drafts folder on Twitter. But that's not what is meant by found poetry. A found poem is when the words exist elsewhere – but crucially, *not already in the form of a poem*. That would be cheating. The words for a found poem might lurk in a marketing email or on the back of a cereal packet, within a Google search engine (as on p. 1) or in a magazine article. The poetry comes in the curation and organisation of the words. There's a long tradition of found poetry. The Dadaists were known in the 1920s for their 'cut-up' poetry, in which existing text from a book or newspaper would be chopped up and rearranged. Similar in nature is blackout poetry, where words are redacted from a section of text, and what remains is your poem.

These days, found poetry is as likely to be derived from online sources; for example, here's a poem I created on Spotify using song titles. I made the poem/playlist for my girlfriend at the time, two days before she left me for a window and door surveyor for Anglia Home Improvements.

Sunday Morning Playlist

Days Like These • I Could Be Happy •
Sunday Morning • The Queen is Dead •
Thinking About You • Last Night •
Can't Get You Out Of My Head •

Dear God • I Should Have Known Better •
Happy Hour • Mistletoe and Wine •
Then • Suddenly • You! Me! Dancing! •
Help! • Mis-shapes • Man Out of Time •

I Can't Stand Up for Falling Down •
You Spin Me Round (Like a Record) •
You Sexy Thing • Falling and Laughing •
Into My Arms • Oh My Lord •

Still Ill • I Say A Little Prayer •
The Drugs Don't Work • Whatever •
Spent the Day in Bed • Close to You •
Beautiful Cosmos • Happy Together •

Found poetry is one of my favourite forms. It shows us that poetry is everywhere: all you need is the time and inclination to go and find it. The next chapter will look at the importance of reading poetry, so let's finish this one with a found poem created out of a selection of unfavourable one- and two-star reviews of my books on Amazon and Good Reads. This was assembled at the suggestion of my therapist, as part of a largely unsuccessful exercise to confront my demons.

Book arrived on time, as described

I didn't buy it myself. I got it as a gift.
I'm not sure what the purpose of this book is.
An introduction to poetry? An attempt at humour?
It generated little interest for me.

If I hadn't run out of books in lockdown,
I don't think I'd have finished it. The poems
are weird, no deep meaning or emotions.
It might be more suited to younger readers.

With banal observations like getting the rubbish bags
out on time, I was going to give it two stars
but spotted a spelling mistake. Clearly written
by a man. Other than that, it's in good shape.

Despite understanding every word and nuance,
I could not muster the tiniest grin.
In summary: it contains few redeemable features.
All the sides and corners are a bit shabby.

A Brief History of Poetry

You may not know it but when you write a poem, you are entering into a conversation with all the poets who have gone before you. Dead poets speak to us across time, and what we write builds on what has gone before, for poetry is rarely created in a vacuum (although it can sometimes be warmed up in an air fryer). As such, we have a duty as poets to be aware of our forebears and the work they have produced. This will not only inspire our own poetry; it helps to situate what we write within a broader historical tradition and, frankly, make it a bit better.*

The only downside to all this is that you have to read other people's poetry, some of which may be quite old. It may contain archaic words, such as 'doth', 'methought' and 'crinkum crankum', or deal with unfamiliar topics, like albatrosses, original sin or a vassal's oath of fealty to his liege. This may force you to turn to reading more recent poetry, enabling you to familiarise yourself with current trends and developments, and to keep tabs on your ~~competitors~~ contemporaries. Try to read widely: seek out the great and classic poems from across time and place, products of different cultures and languages. Where possible, read these poems in

---

* The historical tradition, that is.

their original language: Rumi, for instance, should be read in the original Persian, if you're to fully appreciate all the nuances of his spiritual truths. Few of us have time to learn every language, of course, so I suggest you focus on the key ones: French, Italian, Spanish, Chinese (Mandarin and Cantonese), Japanese, Hindi, Arabic, Latin, Greek (ancient and modern), Hungarian, Russian, Portuguese, Swahili and Australian.

This all may sound a little daunting but I cannot overstate the importance of reading in helping you to develop your own writing abilities. Reading provides us not only with a source of ideas and knowledge, but insights into style, language, voice and experimentation. As you read, you subconsciously consume all manner of useful thoughts, phrases and techniques which you can later pass off as your own. And don't worry, you don't just have to read poetry, you can read more interesting books, too. It all helps in developing your literary ESP.

With so many more appealing distractions to be found in the modern world (TikTok, a new series of *Emily in Paris*, etc.), it can be hard to find the time to read, so it's something you really have to force yourself to do. Be strict with yourself: set aside five or ten minutes at the end of a day in which to drop off on a sofa while reading the same paragraphs you fell asleep to the evening before, or – if you respond well to peer pressure – join a book group and let the fear of being publicly shamed compel you into reading.

Book Group

The last Thursday of every month was Book Group,
when the books would gather together to discuss Brian.

They got straight to the heart of the matter.

'It's no fun here any more,' remarked *Bleak House*, glumly.
'Why doesn't he read us?' whined *The Grapes of Wrath*.
   'It makes me so angry!'

'I don't think I have ever felt so alone,' said *One Hundred Years
   of Solitude*, for whom reality had long since lost its magic.

'Well, I'm sure he only bought me so he can show me off to
   his friends,' complained *Ulysses*, in a stream
   of self-consciousness.

'Consider yourself lucky,' muttered a voice from the Russian
   literature section.
'I bet he can't even remember my name. *The Idiot*.'

'That's because he avoids you like *The Plague*,' said another.
'C'est vrai!' came a cry. 'It is like I do not exist.'

Two shelves below, an atlas shrugged.

'Perhaps he doesn't have time because he spends so much of it
in bookshops?' suggested *Catch-22*.

'He just needs something to sink his teeth into,' declared *Dracula*.
'You're right,' said *Brave New World*. 'Let's not give up on him yet.'

After some *Persuasion*, they agreed to give him one last chance.
'Be quiet!' cried *Waiting for Godot* with *Great Expectations*.
'Here he comes now!'

Brian entered the room, with his phone.

He sat down and watched some videos of baby pandas falling over. After an hour or so, he started googling cats dressed as celebrities.

On the shelf, the books waited with uncracked spines,
their silence speaking volumes.

You will need to read *some* poetry, though. To appreciate it properly, you may have to train yourself to read in a different way to how you might set about the latest Colleen Hoover novel, say, or an article on how to clean your fridge in this month's *Good Housekeeping* magazine. When reading a poem, don't rush at it. Read it once for mood or feeling. Then read it again for mood or feeling, having forgotten to read it for mood or feeling first time around. On your third reading, start to gather some ideas as to what it might be about. Look for words you understand and see if they happen to be situated near to any others you recognise. A short break for a cup of tea and a biscuit is advisable before you embark on your fourth reading. After your fifth or sixth reading, take a look on Wikipedia to see if there's any helpful commentary which might unpack the poem's meaning and shine a light on some of the underlying themes you almost certainly haven't picked up on. After your tenth attempt, briefly consider enrolling on a Critical Reading course with the Open University, before moving on to the next poem.

Given the time commitment involved, you may find it difficult to read more than two or three poems a week. But as you read, you will begin to pick up a sense of not only the individual poems themselves, but poetry as a whole and the long historical tradition which accompanies it. Situating poetry in this broader context is crucial: if we want to see where poetry may take us in the future, we need to understand where it has come from. Or, to save yourself time, you might want to read a potted history of poetry, like the one in the section below, but a bit better.

A Brief History of Poetry

No one knows exactly who invented poetry. Indeed, some scholars believe that poetry had no need to be invented at all, for it was always with us: in the wind and the trees, in the sun and the moon. Other scholars think this is nonsense. What we can say with absolute certainty, though, is that poetry is the world's oldest art form,[*] and one that has captivated humankind since the dawn of time.[†]

It is likely that prehistoric poetry bore little resemblance to the poetry that we know and sometimes love today. There would have been no poems about bin day, for instance, and far, far fewer ones

---

[*] Except for art.
[†] Source unverified.

concerning the need to 'reclaim your wild', given that our earliest ancestors were rather wild anyway. While there may have been no prehistoric TikTok on which those early poems might have gone viral, there were cave walls on which words could be carved for the admiration of the rest of the tribe and the occasional more intelligent bear:

> me carve poem on cave wall
> me hope to be tribe laureate
> but no one know what words me scrawl
> cos language not invent as yet

In those earliest times, poetry was very much an oral tradition; rather than being written down, it would be acted out with the words and stories passed on from generation to generation. The recital of poetry may not have merely been performative, however, but an act which might sometimes be used as a weapon. Bellowed out by invaders during an attack on a rival tribe, the beguiling sounds and rhythms of a poem would make it easier for the assailants to distract the besieged, before dashing their brains out on a nearby rock. This manoeuvre is thought to be the origin of the term 'poetry slam'.

The oldest surviving complete poem is *The Epic of Gargamoth*, believed to have been written around five thousand years ago. Nobody knows where it is from, who wrote it, why it was written, or what audience it was intended for. In that respect, it's very much like poetry shared today on Instagram. We don't even know what the poem says because it was written using one of the world's earliest known alphabets: crudiform script, a code yet to be cracked by language experts. Historically there has been some debate as to whether it might be a poem at all; recent DNA testing on the crudiform pictograms, however, suggests it shares similar genetic characteristics with later poems from this period, most notably in its themes of love, kingship, mortality and slugging it out with monsters.

The earliest named poet on record is Parmathedes of Syracuse, of whose life we know very little, other than that he was from Corinth. We don't know too much about his poetry either as only two words of it have survived,* a fragment still large enough to give rise to a vigorous scholarly debate which has persisted for more than fifty years, most recently in J. A. Aitken's 450-page monograph, 'The Poetry of Parmathedes of Syracuse: A Critical Reappraisal'. What we do know, however, is that by the third century BC, poetry was flourishing; so much so that this period is now widely regarded as the golden age of classical poetry. It reached its apogee in 268 BC when poetry was officially recognised as an Olympic sport. Poets would compete for the honour of 'Laureate', and recite their verses while wrestling naked. It's a tradition which still persists to this day, with the most recent UK poet laureateship won by Simon Armitage, who defeated Wendy Cope in the final with a dramatic reverse bulldog and pin in the bout's closing seconds. The first laureate of them all was Aridodgenes, a Theban poet, now largely remembered for his epic *Goat Song Cycle*,† a sequence of thirty-line love poems to his wife, Cosmina, who had been turned into a goat following a spat with the goddess Artemis. Sadly, of the two hundred poems which comprise his *Goat Song Cycle*, none have survived entirely intact. The most complete is *Goat Song 31*.

---

* 'Θα πρέπει', which translates as 'should I'.
† Incidentally, it is believed that the word 'tragedy' derives from Aridodgenes, the Greek for 'goat song' being tragōidia, from tragos ('goat') and aeidein ('to sing').

Goat Song 31

1 O capricious Artemis,
  Your cruel bow fires a bolt of love
3 Worthy of Eros himself,

  And condemns my heart
  To this dumb creature, who stands
6 On the desolate hillside,

  Staring vacantly back at me,
  A fly dancing upon her brow,
9 Her mouth full of grass.

  But I shall not stand back
  And allow hope to wither on the vine,
12 As if sun-drenched by Helios.

  Come, my cloven-foot lover!
  Let me stroke your strong horns
15 And observe the wisps

  Of your beard wave gently
  In the early evening breeze.
18 Lie down on this mountain slope

  As I
      your coarse, shaggy fur
21 And   in the

Ne'er before have two loved like this!
With great ardour, take my
24   until

        up your
        like a
27   bleat!

        sleep softly
In sweet and tender embrace,
30 Greatest of all time.

Poetry continued to play a prominent role during the years of the Roman Republic and Empire, despite the fact that poets were made to write in Latin. Notable amongst them was Livid, who is celebrated now primarily for his angry, political poems targeted at the emperor and the senate, but who ironically had started off his career as a comic poet.* In AD 26 he wrote his famous 'Tirades', a series of short poetic rants against the political establishment, which was to see him receive the most severe of punishments outside the death sentence: exile to the Isle of Wight.

---

* Most famously, his poem 'Six Ways to Decline Broccoli':
  Broccoli
  Broccolus
  Broccolo
  Broccolum
  Broccolater
  Broccolaaarggh.

Tirade: 58

The careers of politicians
consist of three main positions,
which I shall now supply:
they stand, they sit, they lie.

As the Roman Empire began to crumble towards the end of the second century AD, so did its poetry. In the centuries which followed many of its finest poems were carried off by raiding barbarians, the language-rich stanzas plundered for their words and imagery. Sometimes entire works would be melted down to the base metal of their individual letters, which in turn would be fashioned into bracelets, necklaces and other primitive jewellery. There was a very real possibility that poetry might have died out altogether during this period but it began to re-emerge around 800, mainly in the form of heroic sagas and epic tales, which tended to involve a lot of shouting, maiming and killing, as well as a bit more maiming.

It was to be another four hundred years until poetry was to undergo its next big revolution: the invention of rhyme. Its introduction is credited to John Cowper, clerk to the parish of Salford, in 1349, with what is thought to be the very last poem he was to write:

I Don't Wanna Be Yours

When I met you, it was loathe at first sight
You're as welcome as a fleabite in the night

Because you're the source of all my ills
You give me fever – yeah, and the chills
You're as wanted as a weeping sore
You're the red cross painted on my door
Here, let me spell it out for you, I won't be vague –
You're best avoided like the plague

I don't care if you're exotic
You make me nauseous and necrotic
I've got buboes more attractive than you
You send me gangrene with envy – yeah, it's true
You're a pain in the arse, the arms and the legs
What I'm saying is . . . you're the dregs
From Satan's infernal chamber pot
You've left me in a tight blackspot
Just like my temperature, you're all the rage
You're best avoided like the plague

We've all got our little imperfections
But you're one nasty vile infection
The thought of you makes my lymph nodes swell
I really do not feel too well
You'll be the death of me – and there's the truth
My mortality rate's going through the roof
If the world's a stage, I'd shove you off it
Don't label me a sage or prophet
But I think this could be my last page
I wish I'd avoided you – and the pl

Early modern poetry largely concerned itself with the act of wooing. Lacking an equivalent of Tinder, suitors would spend their evenings shouting poetry beneath the bed-chamber window of a potential lover. Should a poem be received favourably, the curtains would be swiped to the right, and a beckoning finger would encourage its reciter to scale the walls and climb through the window. A swipe of the curtains to the left would inevitably be followed by the poet being struck by a gourd. Despite these risks, love poetry was everywhere; it was the language of the court and commoners alike. Some poets were like pop stars and would tour towns and villages, performing their poems in front of audiences of as many as thirty or forty people – crowds unimaginable to most poets today. Often there would be musical accompaniment to the poems, usually on the lute or mandolin, as was the case for this delightful sixteenth-century love poem, composed by Sir Richard Astleigh, Earl of Newton-le-Willows.

Ne'er shalt thee be given up by me

Thou and I are nay strang'rs to love
Thou knoweth the regiment and so doth I
A fulsome bond is what I am bethinking of
Thou would not receiveth this from any oth'r swain
I just wanteth to bid thee of mine own humour
I shall maketh thee und'rstand

Ne'er shalt thee be given up by me
Ne'er shalt I let thee down
Ne'er shalt I runneth 'round and forsake thee
Ne'er shalt I maketh thee caterwaul
Ne'er shalt I sayeth farewell
Ne'er shalt I bespeak a falsehood and hurt thee

We has't known each oth'r from times of yore
Thy heart aches, but thou art too dainty to sayeth it
Inside, we both knoweth what hast been going on
We knoweth the game and we shall playeth it
And if thee asketh me of mine own humour
Bid me not thou art too blindeth to see

Ne'er shalt thee be giveth up by me
Ne'er shalt I let thee down
Ne'er shalt I runneth 'round and forsake thee
Ne'er shalt I maketh thee caterwaul
Ne'er shalt I sayeth farewell
Ne'er shalt I bespeak a falsehood and hurt thee

In the centuries which followed, poetry continued to be mainly about love and its different varieties: romantic; platonic; unrequited; requited; religious; self; tough; puppy; cupboard. Throw in some poems exploring theological questions and uncertainties, and that's pretty much that lot covered. But everything was to change in the eighteenth century with the arrival of the industrial revolution, a development which was to have profound and long-reaching effects on poetry. Within a couple of decades, most poems were no longer being lovingly handcrafted at home, written by sensitive souls working by candlelight, but were brought into factories and mass-produced on an unimaginable scale. Estimates suggest that the number of poems produced at this time increased from around four thousand in 1750 to more than three million in 1820. The working conditions for poets as they laboured in the factories were appalling: sixteen-hour shifts; cramped and inky workspaces, often having to desk-share; limited access to biscuits; tight restrictions on adjectives, and a complete ban on metaphors. In some factories, children as young as four years old would be involved in the production of verse. Inevitably, quality suffered as the poets struggled to keep up with the demand for cheap, unornamented poetry. In response, the poets organised a strike, the first in a long line of industrial disputes which continues to this day.

The Strike

While the irony was still hot, the poets came out on strike.
In dull, unpoetic prose, they set out their demands:
greater job obscurity; reduced wordloads; improved pensive
    benefits;
a 12% pay increase to combat the rising cost of loafing.

Picket lines and stanzas were set up outside cafes
and writing sheds; in train carriages; beside park benches.
Metaphors were stockpiled, mountains of them,
while the inflation rate of hyperbole soared.

As the protests proliferated, rumours spread that an army
of AI bots would be called up to meet the demand
for meditations on the human condition; for life without poetry
was like a world without birds or flowers.

And so the poets joined forces with the nurses
and the junior doctors and the ambulance workers and the
    teachers
and the rail workers and the postal workers and the civil servants
and the university staff and the environment agency workers

and the passport office staff to march on Westminster,
only to find the government itself had gone out on strike
in protest against all the strikes; had been on strike, in fact,
for six months and more, only nobody had noticed.

A counter-movement to the industrialisation of poetry was provided by the rise of the Romantic poets. These poets sought to return poetry to its pre-industrial status by celebrating stuff like clouds and daffodils, nightingales and skylarks. Willoughby Whitworth was one such poet; in his long poem *The Delude*, he wrote extensively about his relationship with the English countryside. It's a theme he was to return to again and again, such as in this poem from 1794.

Lines Written in Early Summer*

Beloved English countryside,
I ramble through your meadows green
on a fifteen-mile round-trip hike
to the nearest cash machine.

The linnets singing in the trees!
The blackthorn! What a scene! O
such undisturbed, idyllic charm.
I'd love a frappuccino.

And yonder, the workman's cottage.
Grade II Listed. Beams of oak.
Holidaymakers 'neath the thatch
lie awake in fear of smoke.

Held close in Nature's soft embrace,
O how my senses tingle.
I stretch my arms up to the sky
to get a mobile signal.

---

* In recent years, there has been a debate among scholars as to whether this poem was actually written by Willoughby Whitworth. Those who question its provenance point to a number of references to technology of which not even the visionary Whitworth could have been aware in 1794. Some go further still and deny even the existence of Whitworth himself, claiming that he was an imaginary figure created by the notorious late twentieth-century forger of poetry, Talbot Chesterton.

Beloved English countryside –
wild and wondrous, proud and pretty.
So perfect, in every single way,
I just wish it was the city.

Among the Romantic poets, there developed a reputation for drunkenness and debauchery, and in doing so, they contributed to the popular image of the reckless and dissolute poet, their behaviour unpredictable and unruly through drink or drugs. It remains an enduring image, one which Andrew Motion found hard to throw off during his tenure as poet laureate. The financial difficulties created from such heavy drinking would often lead the romanticists to write poems in the form of promissory notes.

Owed to a Grecian Ern

Thank you, Ernesto,
for buying those ouzos.
I guess that must mean
I owe you ten euros.

The Victorian era witnessed further disruption to poetry as moral attitudes changed. Certain words found themselves banned from poems: bosom, throb, moist, engorged, quiver, clitoris. The writing of a dirty limerick might result in a five-year prison sentence or transportation to Australia, where that kind of poetry thrived. In this new puritanical atmosphere, underground poetry clubs sprang up, where poets would swap illicit poems about naughty shenanigans in the Garden of Eden, or having a Prince Albert.

Although wars had existed, it wasn't until the twentieth century that poems about them became fashionable, even though one imagines the war poets themselves must have wished they had not. In the First World War, there was no art form more successful in chronicling the suffering of the combatants and the senselessness which accompanied it than poetry. But it was not long before poetry was to reinvent itself once more with the rise of modernism. Escaping from the straitjacket of formalism, verse unhampered by restrictions of rhyme and meter became the dominant mode. As this made it far easier to write, poetry experienced a new renaissance. It became an era of freedom and experimentation, transforming what had become a staid and formulaic art form into a fresh and vital one for the modern age. When it came to daring and originality, nobody did it better than the avant-garde poet and later convicted felon AA HEMMINGS.

I CARRY YOUR HEART WITH ME

I CARRY YOUR HEART WITH ME(I CARRY IT IN
A BAG)I AM NEVER WITHOUT IT(EVERYWHERE
I GO IT LEAKS,MY DEAR;AND WHATEVER MESS
IS MADE IS YOUR DOING,MY LOVE)
                                        I FEAR
THE POLICE(FOR I ALSO HAVE YOUR LIVER)I WANT
NOTHING(FOR SURELY NOW OUR LOVE IS TRUE)
EXCEPT PERHAPS FOR A BRAND NEW BAG
AND A CHANGE OF CLOTHING, TOO

HERE IS THE BEATING SECRET NOBODY KNOWS
(HERE IN MY HOLDALL) THIS MUSCLE HOLDS ALL
THE HOPE AND WONDER FROM WHICH LIFE FLOWS
(OR FROM WHICH YOURS ONCE DID, MY DARLING)
THAT MY OWN IS HEAVY IS THE ONLY SNAG

I CARRY YOUR HEART (I CARRY IT IN A BAG)

By the 1950s and '60s, in certain, very limited circles, poetry had become cool: it was termed 'the new rock 'n' roll' (which itself was 'the new skiffle'). Poets became prominent in popular culture: Philip Larkin supported The Rolling Stones on their first world tour, reading excerpts from *The Whitsun Weddings*; John Betjeman was immortalised in a series of prints by Andy Warhol; Allen Ginsberg had a brief cameo in *Coronation Street* as a rough and ready beatnik who steals the heart of Elsie Tanner. There were further developments in the 1970s when it was discovered that poets didn't necessarily have to be white or male or heterosexual, and in fact, they never had been only that. This discovery was to cause an instant revolution among poetry publishers, the results of which we are just beginning to see today.

Fast-forward to the present day and again we see the shamanic ability of poetry to reinvent itself for a new generation. We live in the age of 'instapoetry', where poetry gets written and shared online, through social media; in doing so, it's able to garner huge audiences, including readers who never even realised that poetry might hold something for them. Instapoems are characterised by short, direct lines signifying nothing, and quite often look like they've been written on a typewriter.

Love is a Skin

love is a skin
that protects you,
a warmth that spreads
from the tips of your fingers
to your heart

sorry – not love –
glove, i meant glove

All these millennia later, after that precocious troglodyte tentatively wrote those first few lines on a cave wall, it is clear that poetry continues to exert its magical power over its readers. And as for the poets themselves, it's now easier than ever before to get their work out there: one click of a button and off it goes, with the potential to reach thousands, if not millions of readers. But while taking ownership of the means of production is one thing, getting anyone to read the poem you have written and shared is quite another. People have got plenty of other things they should be getting on with. So how do you build that audience, create those readers? It's almost as if we need a new chapter to take a look at that. Yes, why don't we do that: let's start a new chapter right now. We could call it 'How to be Well Read', or something.

How to be Well Read

Every couple of hours or so, I receive a message on Instagram from an aspiring poetry superstar asking me for advice on how to get more followers on social media. They've been writing now for five weeks, they tell me, have shared three brilliant poems along the way, and yet still have only twelve people following them, six of whom are spambots. Where are they going wrong, they ask. In reply, I offer reassurance: be patient, keep plugging away, if people enjoy the poems you write your readership will grow.

This answer is not the one I want to give. What I really want to say is this: stop mithering about metrics. Success or failure in poetry cannot be reduced to a series of key performance indicators. And besides, the drive to write poetry shouldn't stem from the pursuit of fame and stardom, but from the creative impulse itself. Perhaps if you spent less time dreaming about being 'popular', and more thinking about the spark which has been ignited inside yourself, you might be happier. In other words, if the aim of your poetry is to get followers, you're doing it all wrong. I never do respond in that fashion, though – except, I suppose, here in this book, which some people might think is a rather cowardly, passive-aggressive way of going about things, but one that is very much in keeping with my *modus operandi*.

But now I've had time to reflect on what I've written in that last paragraph – over a cup of tea and an episode of *Pointless* – perhaps the answer lies somewhere in the middle. Yes, poets *should* write for themselves, to express what they want to say and satisfy their creative urges, but what poet would not want their work to be read by others, to achieve some kind of recognition, to glow in the receipt of a reader's warm, bosomy embrace? Or their warm, non-bosomy embrace for that matter. For some, a cold, bosomy embrace may also be acceptable; although it must be said that rare is the occasion that a poet will enjoy a cold, non-bosomy embrace.

Regardless, poets are far more likely these days to receive some rudimentary kind of embrace than they used to be. For a long time, the 'general public' (i.e. those people who don't fill their hours writing or thinking about poetry) regarded poetry with suspicion, perceiving it as difficult and inaccessible. It was a situation hardly helped by the poetry community itself, which, in turn, would often regard any poetry which did find itself embraced by the wider public with similar levels of suspicion, if not contempt. There was a disconnect. As Adrian Mitchell wrote, in the preface to his first volume of poems, in 1964: 'Most people ignore most poetry because most poetry ignores most people.' But even more than that, poetry was easy to ignore. Or at least, once you'd left school it was. Physically, you could only encounter it in slim volumes in similarly slim sections of bookshops, situated in their deepest recesses, out of harm's way. To hear a poem, you had to wilfully attempt to do so by tuning into Radio 4 or scouring your local newspaper for information on a 'recital'. But all that has changed. The rise of social media has created a new place for poetry and people to meet. Now poems jostle with jokes and cartoons, videos of cats and dogs, rants about the government or wokeness, photographs of meals or holidays, influencers paid to sell clothing brands or plug restaurants. Even the poets have started to get into the act.

How to Write Poems and Influence People*

Introducing an exciting new collaboration with . . .
the English language,
brought to you in association with The Noun Shack™
and Mme Boucher's Verb Emporium™.

All the words featured in this poem
are available in the 14th edition of *The Chambers Dictionary*
    (£29.99),
your one-stop lexicographical shop for all your logophilic needs.
To get *your* copy: buy one.

For anyone fond of the music of words
and how language is malleable,
Kim Parker's magnificent *How To Make Your Poems Rhyme*
has proved quite invaluable.

Finally, if you've enjoyed, relished or savoured
any of the adjectives featured, presented or displayed in the
    stanzas above,
why not subscribe to *findtherightword.com*
and enter their prize draw/raffle/sweepstake/lottery
to win a year's supply of synonyms.

> * Please note that all views expressed in this poem belong to its author alone.
> and came to me, unbidden, while poolside at the Hotel Tangier:*
> the perfect getaway break on which to contemplate the human condition.

As evidenced above, it's easy to be cynical about social media and I'm very pleased that it is. But social media does show us that a broader, more democratic appetite for poetry exists after all. Some poems even go viral. In 2016, after the terrible news of the murder of the MP Jo Cox, Philip Larkin's poem 'The Mower' was shared on Twitter. The poem is mournful and melancholic but also compassionate and powerful. It travelled around Twitter at lightning speed, bursting out from the bubble of poetry aficionados to find a much broader audience. It was re-shared over 3,500 times and reached a readership of half a million readers in just a few days. Suddenly, thirty-seven years after the poem was written, it was relevant.

And that can be the power of social media for poetry: as a place to share words at the point of need. Social media can lend poetry an immediacy other outlets do not possess; no longer is a poem trapped in the pages of a book on a distant shelf, or patiently

> * When making your reservation, quote BILSTON 26 to receive 20% off your stay.

waiting to be read at a performance taking place two weeks next Thursday. It's there, where readers need it, when they need it. But to maximise the reach of your poetic content, you first need to identify your strategic goals and strategies.

1. Choose Your Market Segment

In the context of social media, the currency of what a poet chooses to write about is important. It's no fluke that I'm able to command such a youthful audience for my own poetry. Over the years, I've learnt how to engage that younger generation by searching out topics that resonate with them, and writing poems that speak to them directly about the issues in their own lives. These are poems written in a language they can understand and relate to, with familiar, immediately recognisable cultural reference points. Here's one, for instance, which went viral with that younger generation, about the 1980s pop icon Paul Young.

Paul Young

it was quite by accident
that i discovered Paul Young
in the garden that morning,
living under a hat

he appeared to have
made himself quite at home there
although he admitted
to periods of abject loneliness

i would visit him daily,
feeding him turnips,
the ends of which
he would store in his turn-ups

upon arriving, he would beg me
to stay for good this time
but having other things to attend to,
i never did

i did enjoy
the feeling of him being near, though,
so every time i went away,
i would take a piece of him with me

then one day, to my dismay,
i lifted up his hat, and found
there was nothing left of him
for me to take

in a rage, i tore his playhouse down
before going inside to play
with my kajagoogoo

Unsurprisingly, the teenagers loved it. The poetry world can sometimes be a little sniffy when it comes to targeting readers in this fashion, but the concept is not a new one. I think it was the early eighteenth-century poet Alexander Pope* who famously wrote:

> 'It is important for the Modern Poet to identify and target key Market Segments in order to optimise potential Revenue Streams and monetise Poetic Content.'

And Pope was quite right about that: it's about finding those topics which marry up with identifiable market segments. While it may grate to write about 'market segments' when referring to the high art of poetry, it has long been the tradition to think in such terms, whether that be Seamus Heaney's targeting of the lucrative agricultural-machinery industry ('Digging', 'Tractors', etc.) or Emily Dickinson and the teenage Emo market ('I am nobody, who are you? Are you nobody, too?').

Once you've undertaken your research and identified the market segment you plan to target (preferably one which not only has the disposable time in which to read your work but enough disposable income to buy a book of it), brainstorm with a pet the potential interests and preoccupations that segment will typically have. From there, draw up a list of topics and then prioritise which poems to write based on maximum potential shares and likes. For example, if your plan is to target couples in their sixties who are members of the National Trust, you might want to focus on poems about the Sunday night joy of *The Antiques Roadshow* and the decline in national educational standards, rather than the latest

---

* Note to self: must check source.

album drop from Charli XCX or the obstacles to owning your own home. Establishing the right topics is key, but to be truly successful you need your poetry to be infused with the kind of imagery to which that market segment can relate. Here, for instance, is an erotic poem aimed at readers in the age 35–55 bracket, suffused in images appropriate to that demographic.

This is Hardchore

Scrub me. Buff me.
Get down on all fours.
Fill me. Stack me.
Rummage through my drawers.

Rinse me. Spin me.
Tumble dry my mind.
Press me. Fold me.
Drape me on your line.

Grout me. Scour me.
Make my fittings gleam.
Bleach me. Teach me.
Squirt your Mr Sheen.

Plump me. Pump me.
Fill my tank with fuel.
Dust me. Suck me
With your crevice tool.

Sift me. Sort me.
Crush me with your weight.
Stuff me. Tie me.
Put me out by eight.

And when it comes to targeting markets, don't be afraid to be ambitious. You may have always wondered, for instance, why so many poets over the centuries have been preoccupied with death. But if you think about it, death is one of the fundamental human experiences: there are none of us whose lives remain untouched by it; there are none of us who will escape it. As such, it represents a lucrative market to the ambitious poet, particularly if you're lucky enough to get one of your poems onto the much-coveted funeral circuit. Take time to analyse the competing poems out there on the subject, and identify gaps in the market. While on the surface, death poetry may seem to be a crowded space, there may be a niche your poem might occupy within it. For instance, I've noticed that a lot of poems about death make the mistake of having been written from a deeply personal perspective, rather than a cool assessment of market needs and requirements. This can mean that they may not be quite appropriate, or 'oven-ready', as it were. Far better for the recently bereaved to have access to a poem that can be customised accordingly to match the unique set of characteristics and circumstances befitting such a solemn occasion.

Requiem for Whoever

It's time now to sleep for the long day is through,
and bright shine the stars in memory of you,
as you slip from this realm into another
but still in our hearts, dear precious a) lover
b) family member c) friend or d) business associate
(please delete as appropriate).

We will carry you with us, your sun will not set –
after all, is there anyone here who could ever forget
your a) thirst for adventure b) generous spirit
c) good sense of humour or d) love of Test cricket.

You were unique; a one-off. But now sadly missed.
You were cherished by all – for who could resist
your a) infectious laughter b) pale blue eyes
c) pencil moustache or d) powerful thighs.

You taught us so much about what's right and what's true,
and I would like to think I've inherited from you
your a) deep sense of justice b) pursuit of perfection
c) devilish good looks or d) record collection.

Without you this planet is a shabbier place.
It's empty and pointless. A profound waste of space.
For cruel Death snatched you from us a) far too soon
b) after a good innings or c) last Tuesday afternoon

and so it is that we are gathered here together
to pay our respects and say goodbye to whoever
in this beautiful a) crematorium b) sacred site
or c) suburban back garden in the middle of the night,

and know that all of us here wish you the best
as you begin your new journey a) to eternal rest
b) to a heavenly realm of joy unalloyed
or c) kicking and screaming into the void.

Level, Tone and Voice

It's not only about subject matter when building that audience: there are considerations of level, tone and voice. Is your poem pitched at an appropriate level for your readers? Is the tone in keeping with someone who really knows that topic, understands it, has lived and breathed it? How authentic is your voice? It's all very well to target potential readers of low- to middle-income UK households in the age 35–60 bracket with a poem about the cost of living crisis, but you need your 'literary deliverable'* to be in tune with that demographic. For example, here are two poems which deal with that topic in very different ways. The first is one of my own.

* poem

The Cost of Loving

I love you more than life itself
but I swear I'll love you better
if you let me turn the heating off
and you wear another sweater.

I cannot get enough of you –
I'm completely in your thrall.
I love to watch you bending over
to unplug the telly at the wall.

Yes, you're the only one for me,
my sweet and fragrant flower –
now you've ditched your daily bath
for one weekly 5-min shower.

Make no mistake, I love you loads,
you send my head into a spin.
Our cycle's set to eco-wash:
let's cram as much as we can in.

My cup of love's full to the brim,
it overflows, my petal.
So make yourself a brew with me,
but don't overfill the kettle.

The next poem is by Toby Salt, self-acclaimed poet and 'flâneur', whatever that is. You may be familiar with Toby Salt, if you've ever attended the Saffron Walden Poetry Festival or are a member of his close family. His work is regularly featured in a number of poetry magazines, such as *Syzygy* and *Impetigo*, and he is currently Poet-in-Residence at Chieveley Services, the motorway service station near Newbury in Berkshire, just off Junction 13 of the M4. Here's his treatment of the cost of living crisis.

Aspidistra Sunset

silent shake of chipped ceramic pig
        not one shekel –
shackled, I haunt the hallway in heliotropic trance
dressed in dead people's clothes

these are my essential goods –
permafrost sleeping bag stuffed with blue withered twigs,
Dimplex heater, broken conch; lame goat
who speaks only   Albanian

o lord, give us this day our quotidian cumquats

christ!   each hour passes like
                a dropped fob –
my pronouns have calcified
a bloodied tongue flaps itself to sleep inside an unwashed
Tupperware
box

while in the cruel curl of night,
the ravens pick at flesh with parcellated contentment –
live laugh lapse languish
poverty grips me
like the tweezers that grasp
an unruly nasal hair

& everything
                                    is dying now
the grave wears her green dress
& I sleep with an axe beneath my pillow
to dead head my dreams

too late, it is far too late –
I watch my own face disappear under dark water
the bubbled cry
the long silence

    The first of these two poems was retweeted several hundred times on Twitter, described by somebody called Hayley5621 as 'corking', and was the privileged recipient on Facebook of a tears of joy emoji by Dave B in Harpenden. In contrast, Toby Salt's poem failed to strike a chord on social media and was retweeted only twice (once by the author himself and once by his publisher, Shooting from the Hip Press). It did, however, win the Bishendon Poetry Prize (£250) and was described by the leading poetry journal *Calliope* as 'a *tour de force*, the poem which says more than any other about what it is to be human in the dehumanising world of late capitalism'. Salt himself went on to adapt the poem, in the form of a libretto for a three-act opera, co-written with the distinguished contemporary composer Grant Birtwistle.

Now, to be clear, I am not trying to make any particular point here about the relative merits of each poem. I simply think it interesting for us to compare the differences in level, tone and voice you might encounter across poems, and what that might mean by way of popular or critical acclaim. You might have your own view on which of the two poems speaks to you more, such as the first one most probably, and who am I to persuade you otherwise? Maybe you feel the second poem is unnecessarily difficult, wilfully obscure and knowingly pretentious, like much of Toby Salt's work, I really don't know: the object of the exercise is not to judge but merely to ponder quietly and reflect. Some of you, I suppose, might bring into question the very legitimacy of awarding prizes for poetry. Might it be considered demeaning (or 'déclassé', as Toby Salt might say) for art to be forced to compete in that way? Is it right for Toby Salt's poem to be treated as if it was nothing more than some freakishly shaped giant marrow at the annual village show? And besides, how far does £250 get you these days: for a poet like Toby Salt, it wouldn't be enough to keep him in oat milk mocha lattes for more than a week. And who knows, maybe a few of you might even be moved to write a passive-aggressive poem in response to Toby Salt, such as this anonymous one I stumbled across earlier on the c:\ drive of my laptop.

Neither Here Nor There

as you describe
how your work explores
the liminal space

which exists
beyond spatial or ontological
specificities,

I find myself
exploring the liminal space
which exists

between consciousness
and sleep

    These are all excellent reflections, and I would encourage you to keep having them.

O reader, where art thou?

One additional consideration: the geography of your readers. Are you writing primarily for a UK audience? Or is your poem even more focused: on the people of Stoke-on-Trent, for example, or the woman in the purple velour tracksuit who has just moved into number 29? Perhaps you hope for your poem to have broader international appeal. If that's the case, proceed with care for most poetry does not travel well: John Betjeman is rarely read in Azerbaijan, D. H. Lawrence made few inroads in Kuwait, Carol Ann Duffy has no readers in Banbury. Specific cultural references may baffle readers in other countries: what is a 99 ice cream, someone in Papua New Guinea might ask; a Ugandan reader may never have heard of Vernon Kaye. Even when there may be fewer cultural obstacles, there may be a language barrier, such as between the UK and the US.

Separated by a Common

Dear American English (honourable neighbour),
Please excuse my bad behaviour,
I don't want to throw a spanner
but let's no longer labour in pretence –
you're all talk and no trousers,
you simply make no sense.

What's harboured beneath your bonnet –
crikey, an encyclopaedia could be written on it
with all its uncivilised features!
It's a catalogue of misdemeanours,
a centre for wrongly spelt endeavours,
enough to fill a car park.

Now, I don't mean to show ill-humour,
but I've heard this rumour
you think I'm rubbish, a failure
to be rubbed out with your 'eraser'.
Careful – I'm no dummy. I wouldn't risk it.
You really do take the biscuit.

But what use throwing petrol onto fire?
You're Spring, I'm Autumn, you see.
How crisp and golden are my leaves –
let's agree to disagree.

With love,
English

Language

Dear English (honorable neighbor),
Please excuse my bad behavior,
I guess this must be something of a wrench
but let's no longer labor in pretense –
the words you speak are utter pants,
you simply make no sense.

What's harbored beneath your hood –
jeez, only an encyclopedia could
contain all its unmodernized features!
It's a catalog of misdemeanors.
a center for wrongly-spelled endeavors,
of which there are a lot.

Now, I don't mean to show ill-humor,
but I've heard this rumor
you think I'm trash. You'd like to take
your 'rubber' to me. Big mistake!
I can play the role of pacifier, yet
I'm one tough cookie, don't forget.

But such gassing gets us nowhere.
I don't want you to fall out with me.
Remove that chip from your shoulder –
let's agree to disagree.

With love,
American English

It may be that your poetry will fare better in translation, but even then it is best to proceed with caution. A selection of my poems were once translated into Russian by somebody who came to me highly recommended by the International School of English School in Basingstoke. What's more, he offered very competitive rates. The subsequent book was published in Russia to a tranche of hugely positive reviews. It was only after having shown the collection to a native Russian speaker that I realised how poorly rendered my poems had been. For instance, here's the original English version of my poem 'You Took the Last Bus Home'.

you took
the last bus home
don't know how
you got it through the door

you're always doing amazing stuff

like the time
you caught that train

Here's the translation which appeared in the Russian edition:

Ты взял его.
Последний автобус идет домой.
Я не знаю как.
Это невозможно, чтобы он прошел через дверь.

Всегда делаешь удивительные вещи

Как Владимир Владимирович Путин
На коне.

And here's apparently how that Russian version translates back into English:

You have taken it.
The last bus goes home.
I do not know how.
It is impossibility for bus to go through door.

Always you are doing amazing stuff

Like Vladimir Vladimirovich Putin
On horse.

Building your community

Having identified your market segment and written some poems for it, you now need to build your community. Over time, you will develop your knowledge as to where your 'tribe' are most likely to hang out on social media. Poems about moths, for instance, tend to fare best on Instagram, whereas poetry for the dairy farming community tends to get most traction on Facebook, particularly around 7.30 a.m. when they're having their midmorning tea break. Threads is brilliant for poems about existential dread; BlueSky for poems about Twitter. Twitter, on the other hand, isn't good for anything much at all these days. It's become a far nastier place over the last couple of years but I can't quite put my finger on the reason why. Anyway, here's another poem.

Billionaire in a Midlife Crisis

He's swapped designer jeans and flashy cars
For designer spacesuits and trips to Mars
Where he watches Earth turn on its axis
With its stupid people paying taxes
He's coming down with astro-spend-eritis
He's a billionaire in a midlife crisis

He's got plans to end world poverty
Once his new hair's lost its novelty
He's dropping rap tracks and dissing pronouns
His kids have names they cannot pronounce
He's choosing who his next young wife is
He's a billionaire in a midlife crisis

He's an outspoken champion of free speech
With a mute button in easy reach
He's building an army of online abusers
More spambots equals more X-users
Cause he's been left too long to his own devices
He's a billionaire in a midlife crisis

Less artful dodger, more artless doge
With a pair of jackboots in his wardrobe
And a baseball cap from Marine Le Pen
That says Make the Far Right Great Again
If truth be told, he's not the nicest
He's a billionaire in a midlife crisis

The Nazi salutes? Don't misunderstand –
He'd be the first one to put up his hand
To say no harm meant, it was just a joke
From a humble tech-bro's war on woke
He's full of such self-sacrifices
He's indulging all his whims and vices
He'll buy anything no matter what the price is
Perhaps he's compensating for what his size is
He's a billionaire in a midlife crisis

To establish a community on social media, you need to do more than post a poem every few days. You need to be an active participant, interact with others on the platform and pretend to be interested in what they have to say. Follow other struggling poets and agree to say nice things about their poems in return for kind comments about your own. Seek out minor celebrities, such as the actor and singer Robson Green, and leave comments on their posts about how much you admire them. Should somebody inadvertently share one of your poems with their own followers, take the time to thank them and see if you can find out their address to send them flowers, or write them a love poem such as this one.

I will follow you

I will follow you
'til the end of time,

when worlds explode
and stars go black,

and the whole universe
goes in on itself;

assuming, that is,
you follow me back.

If you engage with social media regularly in such an open and non-cynical fashion, it's possible to build up a following of seventy or so people in just three or four years. What's more, you will have established what publishers refer to as a 'platform' for your poetry, which you can now monetise. But only in a nice way, like this.

Monetisation

The advert said
MONETISE YOUR FOLLOWERS
so he thought
he would respond

by painting them
in the changing light,
like waterlilies
in a pond.

Getting out there

If the frontier of the virtual (and unvirtuous) is not for you, you could always try sharing your poetry with actual people, in a place which has become known as 'the real world'. Go back a few decades and the thought of an evening of poetry – or for that matter, an afternoon of poetry – would instil most right-minded people with horror, akin to Chinese water torture or having to hear about a dream your friend had the previous night. Poetry would often be delivered from an armchair in an incoherent mumble or monotone, punctuated by lengthy awkward silences and sips of Gordon's London Dry Gin disguised as mineral water. Fast-forward to the present day and you'll find poets strutting across the stage like rock stars, swirling microphones above their heads between stanzas, falling to their knees as they deliver that devastating and dramatic last line. The staid and sterile poetry reading of the past has been transformed into a series of miniature one-act plays packed with emotion and drama, without a slender, slip-jacketed book or trembling sheet of paper in sight. Yes, there remain a few poets who might imagine nothing more horrible than having to exhibit such extroversion, but there is no denying that 'performance' has become an increasingly helpful arrow in the twenty-first-century poet's quiver, and it may be as well to focus some of your energy on perfecting your stagecraft.

Reading poems on a stage can be a lot harder than it looks. Some say it's the ultimate human challenge, so here are a few top tips to help you prepare:

1. Rehearse. In fact, whenever you're writing a poem, regardless of whether you ever intend to perform it in public, read it out loud. In the process, you'll identify lines which don't quite work, rhythms or rhymes which need fixing, words which may be difficult to pronounce, like 'otorhinolaryngologist' or 'vicissitude'.

2. Think about your 'set'. When you're on stage, you're a pop star: your poems are your songs, their language is your music. Identify your hit singles, the crowd-pleasers and toe-tappers, and sprinkle them across your set. Intersperse with album tracks and the odd new experimental composition. In doing so, think about the journey on which you are sending your audience, how the poems flow, the light and shade they cast. Juxtapose a serious poem with some comic relief. Remember, what you're really trying to do is to keep the audience awake. To that end, consider shouting every other poem or adding sound effects, such as thunder claps or occasional cannon fire.

3. Find an icebreaker poem within your repertoire to get the audience on your side from the get go. Alternatively, save time on housekeeping notices by incorporating them into your opening poem:

Emergency Procedures

Ladies and gentlemen, I ask for your full attention
as we review the emergency procedures for tonight's performance.

There are two emergency exits in this theatre.
Take a minute to locate the one nearest to you.
Familiarise yourself with it
in the knowledge that my best poetry may be behind me.

Should you experience a sudden loss of interest in tonight's performance,
stay calm, while glancing surreptitiously at a video on your phone
of a dog doing yoga with its owner.

Poetry-cancelling headphones will also drop down from above your seat.
Place the headphones over your ears, like this, and adjust for comfort.

If you are attending this performance with children, please ensure
you do not make that mistake again.

In the unlikely event of a poignant or thought-provoking poem,
please leave your cynicism behind.

Such a poem will serve as a life raft,
providing the emergency lighting you require
to find your way out of a challenging situation.

At this point, I would also ask you to make sure
all your pre-conceived notions of what entertainment is
are stowed away safely during my flights of fancy.

Any emotional baggage should be stored either under the seat in front of you
or preferably, in a distant, hard-to-reach compartment of your brain.

And please note that smirking is prohibited for the duration of the performance.

Finally, while you wait for the next poem,
please take a moment to review all the life decisions you have made which have culminated in your attendance here this evening.

Thank you.

4. Work on the 'bits in between the poems' and how to get from one poem to another. You could read one after another without pause but the audience might appreciate some relief from all that poetry. Instead, introduce your poem, mention how, why or when you wrote it and things they might look out for in it. If it's intended to be a humorous poem, let the audience know in advance what the funny lines are, so they know when to laugh.

5. Decide upon the poem you want to end with. How do you want your audience to go home at the end of the night? Inspired and uplifted? Thoughtful and reflective? Angry and resentful? Puzzled and confused?

6. Think about the physical aspects of your performance. Are you going to swashbuckle around or hug the microphone? Is there an attractive member of the audience you could invite on stage and read a love poem to? Is there an opportunity to crowd-surf?

Which of your three cardigans might you wear? Practise pouting, the raising of a quizzical eyebrow, looking thoughtfully into the mid-distance.

7. Be confident! Your poems might not be very good, but they're *your* poems and no one knows them as well as you, so there is that, I suppose.

8. If you're still nervous, find strategies to help you feel in control of the situation. The first time I ever read my poems in public, it was as a plenary speaker at the annual meeting of the British Naturist Association.

On Delivering My Inaugural Address to the British Naturist Association

To help me
feel more
composed,

I picture
the audience
clothed.

9. Finally, ask yourself what's the worst that could happen. You get jeered at and struck by a tub of red pepper houmous which an audience member has smuggled in to snack on at the interval? You lose your bearings and fall off the stage, fracturing your hip? Somebody records you corpsing on stage and the video

goes viral on social media? Your self-confidence and belief in your poetry are entirely obliterated? Nothing you can't cope with.

10. It would be good to have another tip to share here and bring the total to ten, a nice round number, but I can't think of anything else, I'm afraid.

Getting Published

There remains one other way to find an audience, quaint and as old-fashioned as it may be: get yourself published. It's every poet's dream but far more easily said than done. Or written than done, I suppose, because I wrote that last sentence rather than speaking it, and I wrote it very easily, unlike this one which has begun to ramble somewhat but has now thankfully ended.

It is estimated there are approximately eighty million people currently writing poetry in the UK, all trying to get themselves published – so how do you make your collection stand out? Although there are lots of different kinds of publishers out there, they are all looking for one thing: not poetry. They'd prefer a crime novel, to be honest. One of those so-called 'cosy' ones like Richard Osman's would be good. For some reason, possibly commercial, the prospect of selling three hundred copies of a book, mainly to the poet's friends and family (including a bulk deal back to the author of two hundred and fifty copies), is not an enticing one for a publisher. They may, however, be interested in your work if you have:

1. A 'platform'. You may remember this word from earlier. It's not an actual platform like a dais or the sort of thing you might stand on while waiting for the 7.45 to Matlock Bath. This is publisher-speak for having a readymade audience for your poetry, in order to save them the time of having to do any work themselves. As we've seen, social media is the most obvious way of building one. Other options include blackmail and cyber-terrorism.

2. Critical acclaim. A proven track record of winning poetry competitions and having work published in cutting-edge poetry magazines and journals, such as *Well-Versed*, *Calliope* and *Colophon*, will help your cause. Get known on 'the scene' by attending poetry festivals: you may be able to further your reputation in the field by buying more established poets drinks at bars and offering to carry their satchels for them.

3. £800. There can be a stigma attached to vanity publishing but at least it helps get your work out into the world. Please do be aware that this price does not include copyediting, typesetting, proofing, printing, marketing, sales or distribution.

But let's allow ourselves to dream a little. Imagine, as preposterous as it may be, there are a host of publishers jostling with each other for the privilege of being able to publish your work. To decide which one is the best fit for you, ask yourself a few basic questions. Do they publish authors you might read yourself? If it's a big publisher, might your work get lost among all their blockbuster books and authors? If it's a small publisher, how will they get your book into shops and under the noses of reviewers and potential purchasers? And perhaps most critically of all, how regularly might they take you out for lunch, and does that include pudding, too?

Perspective

I would rather be
a big fish
in a little pond

than a big pond
in a little fish.

Let's take that dream a little further now. You've selected your publisher and they're eager to bring out a collection of your poems. You are now faced with the issue of how to organise it. It's a not dissimilar process to putting together a setlist for when you go on stage. You need to start with an absolute banger, so begin your collection with one of your strongest poems. This helps to lull the reader into thinking the whole collection will be as good as that one. You may want to end with a strong one, too, should a potential purchaser be flicking through it casually and want reassurance that the quality of the collection remains consistent. Your worst poems, the ones which perhaps really shouldn't be published at all, you should slip in between pages 18 and 35 and again between pages 55 and 75. With any luck, your readers may not even get that far through the book to encounter them. Think again about the light and shade through the collection and be careful to ensure that any lines you have which are repetitive have enough distance from each other for the reader not to notice, like I've done here with the final line of the poem on page 93 and the last line of the second stanza on page 189. To maximise sales of your book, you might even consider pretending it's not a poetry collection at all. You could hide your poems inside another kind of book entirely; I don't know, like a diary perhaps, or some kind of introduction about how to write poetry.

To continue the fantasy . . . you've done it! You've written some poems. People love them. You get yourself a publisher. You put together a collection. Your publisher takes those poems, copyedits and typesets them, then prints them in the form of a book, which is sent out into the world. You hold your breath and wait for the adulation and accolades to come flooding in. You keep holding your breath. You begin to turn blue in the face so you let your breath out but that doesn't alter the fact that no one seems to have even noticed your book: it's not been reviewed anywhere; it's only in a handful of bookshops; Sara Cox hasn't called you up to ask if you want to go on that programme about books on BBC2; you notice that copy you gave to your mum on the shelf in her local Oxfam. You feel utterly miserable and wonder why you bothered with any of this poetry business at all. But then your publicist calls. She tells you not to despair, that your book has been noticed after all, and the very next day there will be a review of it in a major daily newspaper. *This is it!* you think. *At last!* You set your alarm early, rush out to buy the paper and, after having spent twenty-five minutes rifling through its pages to locate the review, you finally find it: it's three lines long and they hate it.

The above story has never happened to me, of course, but it might well happen to you. Feelings of insecurity, paranoia, anger, resentment and jealousy are perfectly natural when it comes to publishing a book, and you will draw on all of these in your poetry in the years to come. As for criticism, heed the words of Kingsley Amis: 'A bad review may spoil your breakfast,' he wrote, 'but you shouldn't allow it to spoil your lunch.' Easy for Kingsley to say, you might think; he was probably at Bertorelli's, tucking into pan-fried calves liver with sweet onions, pancetta and parsnip mash, while you're sat on a wall in a supermarket car park eating a £4.99 meal deal, but regardless, there is some sense in it.

One Star Reviewer

The relationship of writer and critic
is, in essence, parasitic –
while one delivers tangibles,
the other grinds its mandibles.

Regard criticism as the price you pay for sticking your head above the parapet and daring to write a book. Don't forget that critics get paid more for writing negative reviews so it's in their interest to say mean things – and the mean things they say come naturally to them because they were probably bullied a lot at school and don't have any friends. Also, never look at any reviews of two stars or fewer on Good Reads and Amazon; they have probably been left there by rival poets or people you have upset in real life.

Publishing a book is not a uniformly awful experience, there can be the occasional benefit. For one thing, it gives you a ready-made excuse to hang around in bookshops.

Never Judge a Bookshop by its Cover

It may call itself a bookshop, but don't be fooled by that.
There may be books in the window, on the tables and shelves,
but really, it's a travel agent selling all-immersive holidays,
weekend breaks, first-class tickets to other worlds,

with a low carbon footprint. It's a pharmacy as well,
dispensing medicines, pick-me-ups, balms: *if symptoms persist,*
please consult your local bookseller; it's a tailor's, offering
a made-to-measure service to achieve the perfect fit;

and a hardware store, with a range of empowering tools
to fix you up, recharge your batteries, switch on lightbulbs.
Its walls are lined with treasure as valuable as any jeweller's,
and twice as bright. Spines shine gold, silver, sapphire, emerald;

there are diamonds amongst them. It's a garden centre,
a place where ideas get planted and a thousand stories bloom,
and a greengrocer, selling fresh, locally sourced produce,
as vital as your five-a-day and more readily consumed.

It's a multiscreen cinema. Peek behind the curtain
of each jacket and you'll find a movie waiting silently to begin.
A stationer's supplying notepads, reams of paper,
with the words already filled in

to save you both the time and bother. A wholefood store
and a fast-food joint. A cosy haven from the cold.
A friendly, family restaurant: *Today's special will revive*
a flagging spirit and restore a lagging soul.

It's a tourist information centre equipped with maps
and helpful guides to steer us on our way.
A busy square in which a whole town gathers
or just a place to hold the world at bay

for a few untroubled stolen minutes. It's itself,
and yet it's something larger, a universe so vast
you could spend ten thousand lifetimes there –
it may call itself a bookshop, but don't be fooled by that.

Poetry sections can be hard to locate in bookshops, but are usually found on a shelf between 'Self-help' and 'Transport'; ironically so, given that poetry can be used as a form of self-help and also transport us to new places. Given the restrictions on budgets and shelf space, it can often be the case that your book is either hidden away or not stocked at all but, fear not, there are a number of strategies you can employ to encourage a shop to give more prominence to your title:

1. When no one is looking, turn your book around so it is face out. You may have to cover up some of the other poetry books in the process.

2. Better still, smuggle your book out from the poetry section and place it on one of the display tables near to the till point. In order to make space, it may be necessary to remove one of the existing titles on that table, preferably a Jeremy Clarkson or David Walliams.

3. Visit the bookshop daily – in a series of different disguises – and ask the bookseller whether they have your book in stock. You may want to mention that you heard somebody talking about it on Radio 4 and saying how good it was. If they have it in stock, purchase that copy as a way to keep an eye on the efficiency of their re-ordering processes. Once you have purchased your own book twenty or thirty times, they may add it to their 'core stock' of poetry titles.

4. Keep an eye out for any rival poets who are attempting to do any of the above, and tell the bookseller you suspect them of shoplifting.

In the course of your book promotion, it may be necessary to involve yourself with large, unscrupulous online booksellers, too. If so, consider their questionable labour practices, impact on smaller businesses and disruption of the books industry. Then remind yourself of the role that independent bookshops can play at the heart of a community and write a poem illustrating why they're so much better.

Advanced Book Search

'I can't remember what it's called
but I'm pretty sure it has a green cover.
What I do know is that the author's name
starts with a P. Or possibly a K.
One of the consonants, definitely.

She was talking about it on Radio 4 last week –
although now I come to think of it,
it may have been Radio 2. On Monday.
It's a novel. Set in Bridgend, if that helps.
No, hang on . . . Bridport. Or Brisbane?
She did sound Australian, in a Welsh kind of way.

At least, I think it's a novel. It might be
an autobiography. Or a travel guide.
But I am certain it has a green cover
because I saw a picture of it
in the newspaper a few weeks ago,
although that could have been another book . . .'

are words that take a long time to type
into an online search box,
and lead to unsatisfactory results.
I ask my local bookseller instead,
who fetches the book from the shelf.
Turns out the cover was red.

Let's Get Practical

Being a poet is not all fun and games. It is, in fact, very little of either. The hours are long, the workload unwieldy, the rewards uncertain. A recent estimate suggests that the average poet will spend approximately 45% of a typical working day staring into space; 26% looking at their phone; 18% doing inconsequential admin; 9% making tea; and only 2% doing any actual writing. It is little wonder that, historically, poets have carried a reputation for being disorganised, unreliable and dissolute. Think of Coleridge being awoken from his opium slumbers by the man from Porlock, or that time Philip Larkin assigned the wrong Dewey decimal code to a handbook of social epistemology. Chaos and disorder have woven themselves together to form the mythology of the tortured poet: too tormented by their poetic genius to bother with reliability, sobriety or punctuality.

Riddle

he was a riddle
wrapped up in a mystery
inside an enigma
inserted into a conundrum
clothed in a puzzle
hiding inside a question mark

as a consequence,
the poet was twenty minutes late
for his hair appointment

But for the contemporary poet, such qualities are neither desirable nor sustainable: the emergence of AI and an army of evil poetry bots have put paid to that. In these times, laureates cannot rest on their laurels, no matter how restful and comfortable their laurels may be. It's all very well going about life with a rakish insouciance and Byronic flair, but if you can't organise yourself to get your new poem for International Cheese Day onto Twitter before some poetry bot beats you to it, you're not going to get very far.

The life of a poet is often a solitary one (not by design, they just tend to not have many friends or be able to form meaningful relationships) and so the responsibility for knuckling down and getting on with it lies at the poet's cedar-clad writing-shed door alone. So let's look at some of the techniques to keep you on track and focused, and it all starts with a list. A set of objectives is as important for the poet as it is for the global logistics supervisor or digital solutions engineer. Get into the habit of writing a To Do

List for the day ahead, remembering to ensure that your objectives are SMART:

Specific
Measurable
Achievable
Realistic
Tea, lots of tea.

Here, for example, is one of my own To Do lists for a typical day of poetry business.

To Do List

- delay; defer; equivocate
- make some tea; procrastinate
- look at Twitter; stroke the cat
- readjust the thermostat

- dawdle; dither; hem and haw
- fill the kettle; chew my jaw
- write nine words; spin on chair
- play six games of solitaire

- observe the merry, dappled light
- dancing on the page of white
- review my words; paper scrunch
- stroke the cat; break for lunch

- prioritise new tasks to shirk
- ponder changing world of work
- look at Twitter; spin on chair
- make a brew; loiter; stare

- check out latest cricket score
- reorganise the kitchen drawer
- write nine words; cross six out
- stroke the cat; stoke self-doubt

- make tea; stroke cat; cricket; stare
- Twitter; chair-spin; solitaire
- stroke tea; make cat; twicket; wallow
- write To Do list for tomorrow

Even with such a detailed plan of action, it can be easy to become distracted. Built into the job spec for a poet (or Poetic Content Creator as it is more commonly becoming known) is the requirement to do a lot of thinking: an act which can sometimes be indistinguishable from not doing very much at all. In such conditions, idle fancies and inconsequential daydreams flourish. Your mobile phone can be particularly unhelpful in this regard, not only as a distraction but, with so much going on in the world, it can put you in a very distressed state of mind.

doomscrolling

the whole day scrolling
through all that misery,
pain and heartache,

wretchedness and despair,
anxiety and torment,
hardship and unhappiness,

until – finally! – I get to it.
1970 – the year of my birth.
I fill in my card details

& await confirmation
of my tickets for An Evening
with Mike Tindall, MBE

Then there's the temptation of Wordle and Quordle. And Octordle, of course, plus Crosswordle and Worldle. Not to mention Durdle and Dawdle, Birdle and Curdle (today's answer: lemon, yet again). You may claim these games serve as short, fun exercises to get your brain warmed up, to facilitate the pumping of a few preliminary words around your poetic circulatory system, but you're only kidding yourself. My advice would be to spend no more than two to three hours on these activities, and keep your phone locked up in another room for the rest of the working day. Except, that is, for those occasions when you might need it for some poetry-related research: to look up potential words in an online rhyming dictionary, for instance, or to investigate who was the Greek goddess of the moon for some clever allusion, or to visit a price comparison website for office stationery. Given that you will be needing your phone a lot with all this research, you might want to make sure you lock it up in a room very near to where you are working, or better still just keep it on your desk next to you, to save yourself time.

If you *should* happen to glance at that phone, though, and inadvertently doomscroll for several hours, it can make it very hard to get back to the poem in hand. With all the nastiness of the world weighing down upon you, it's no wonder fresh words are not forthcoming. In such circumstances the best thing you can do is to take a break. Get up from your desk, put on your boots or Crocs, and head outside. Spending time in nature can lead to huge benefits for both your mental and physical well-being, which in turn will foster more inspiration and creativity for your poetry. New scientific research suggests that poets are 42% more productive having first wandered lonely in open green space. Proximity to nature releases in our brains a chemical called rhymatocin, which quite literally gets our creative juices flowing and enables us to think more profoundly about the human condition.

Escape into Nature

There are times when it all gets too much
and I have to switch off the TV and the radio
and my brain, and escape outside.

I say good afternoon to next door's dog.
Have you seen the latest about the government, he barks,
you couldn't make it up. I smile weakly

and make my excuses before walking on
past the pub, whose sign creaks in protest
against the steep rise in the cost of living.

From the tall branches of the tree opposite,
a seminar is in progress; a squirrel sets out
his ideas about how to alleviate the refugee crisis

while a chaffinch flaps his wings angrily.
It all gets too much for one leaf, who hurls
itself down, remembering Trump.

I feel the eyes of a murderous-looking crow
upon me, annoyed about global warming no doubt,
and make my way quickly down to the river

where – for a few precious, stolen moments –
I close my eyes and listen to the water
as it laps gently against the bank

until I hear the slap of wet feet approaching.
Thought I'd find you here, the duck quacks,
Now what the hell we gonna do about Putin?

Where you choose to write can be very important, too. If you are unfortunate enough to share a house with other people, you may need to adopt strategies to head off any interactions with them. A glazed, faraway look in your eyes will only get you so far; sometimes not even close family members will recognise that as a sign that you are not to be disturbed. Fraternisation with other human beings can result in disastrous consequences for your poetry.

Distraction

My train of thought
has been cancelled
and a replacement bus service
is in operation.

If possible, find the most remote room in the house, attach a large DO NOT DISTURB sign to the door, then lock and bolt it securely. If appropriate, the addition of barbed wire can also send out the right message while serving as an attractive, decorative steel festoon. To avoid the possibility of having to talk to someone should you need to emerge from the room for urgent toileting business, consider equipping your space with a small portable convenience.

Comfort Zone

Please take note:
this is my designated comfort zone.
All patrons are kindly requested
to leave me alone.

Please refrain from using your phone.
Do not knock upon my door.
Do not cross the yellow line
I have painted on the floor.

Should you need to contact me –
if you really must insist –
leave a message with my secretary,
who does not exist.

How you choose to organise your desk is entirely a matter of personal preference. Famously, Albert Einstein is said to have had a sign on his desk which read: 'If a cluttered desk is an indication of a cluttered mind, then what does an empty desk indicate?' – although because his desk was in an absolute state, nobody ever saw the sign, which had become buried beneath all his books and papers, dirty mugs and bowls of half-eaten pasta. My own preference is for a largely bare surface containing few objects, save for three pencils, a biro, a marker pen, a set of highlighter pens (pastel colours only), five sheets of paper, a set square and protractor, a laptop, my phone, five notebooks, a small pile of defunct coins from across Europe, a clump of receipts from March to September 2023, three leaky AAA batteries, a key for a lock of no known location, a badge containing a picture of René Magritte's 'Ceci n'est pas une pipe', a half-eaten packet of custard creams, five mugs (two containing tea, both cold), a yellow plectrum, a voucher (expiry date: 21st January 2019) for up to £12 off my next food bill at The Greyhound in Bessels Leigh, near Abingdon, two mouldy conkers, a miniature desktop football table and a cat.

How Not to Organise Your Desk

After I heard there was a hierarchy
we subconsciously use
when we apply adjectives to a noun –
opinion, size, age, shape, colour,
origin, material, purpose –

I sat there at my square, honey-brown, little, writing, oak, old desk,
and marvelled at the hidden intricacies
of the English amazing language.

The matter of your chair should also be given serious thought. Avoid a seating solution which is too comfy: a comfy bottom is a comfy mind, one apt to give rise to safe, unadventurous poetry. You may also find yourself dropping off to sleep at frequent intervals, particularly during spells of heavy thinking. But don't choose a seat which is too hard and unforgiving either; remember that you're going to be sat on it for long periods, a prospect which is depressing and miserable enough as it is.

Some poets prefer not to be stuck behind a desk. They would rather be outside, engaging with the world that surrounds them, their creativity sparked by the space through which they move. I admire anyone who can write on the go like that, but it's worth being aware of some of the hazards which can result. The poem below, for instance, was originally conceived as an attempt to capture the many and varied scenes passing by my window on a train journey from Oxford up to Manchester.

Scenes from a Train Window

A pylon looms up suddenly like a sini-
Two birds puncture the early morning blue as th-
Cows stare into the distance and wonde-
Fields sleep drowsily, waiting for-
Buddleia bubbles up along the tr-
A woman waves at her youn-
Some buildings.
Graffiti.
Wolverhampton Railway Station.

As mentioned before, don't forget to take your trusty notebook with you when you're out and about. But try to be realistic. While it's always helpful to jot down thoughts and ideas, words and phrases as they come to you, it takes a very experienced poet to write an actual poem when on the go like that. Poetry in motion is not so straightforward in practice. It was a lesson I learnt the hard way. When I first began to write poetry, I would walk along the street, tapping words into my phone as I made my way to the office each morning. It wasn't always successful.

The Problem with Writing Poems as You Walk to Work

writing poems
as you walk to work

can be tricky
in the morning murk

the thing you need
to mind the most

is bumping into
a lam

The weather can prove to be a challenge, too. Windy, blustery conditions are notoriously difficult in which to write. If you do find yourself attempting a poem when you're out on such a day, my recommendation would be to steer clear of light verse and favour words of weight and substance.

The Problem with Writing Poems on a Windy Day

The problem   y
with writing poems
on a windy day –   a

no sooner
do you get the words down   w
then they just   a
            w
b   l   o

    Temperature can also play havoc with getting your words down correctly. Poetry is best written at room temperature and, unless you are Edgar Allen Poe, should not be served chilled. Writing at colder temperatures can affect not only the speed at which you are physically able to write but the sluggishness of your brain. And matters don't improve in the heat either.

The Problem with Writing a Poem in Hot Weather

The problem
with writingpoems
inhot weather

isthatthe words
getsweaty
and sticktogether.

Although the pace of an average day for a poet could be described as somewhere between glacial and tortoise, there are always times when you need to put a shift in. It could be that the muse is upon you* and the words are spewing out of you uncontrollably with no end in sight, or more likely, it's because you have a deadline from your publisher which you've ignored for the last six months with the consequence that you now need to write forty-five poems in a twenty-four hour period. In such circumstances, it can be tempting to resort to artificial stimulants to keep you going through the night. Abusing your body for your art has its dangers, though, and the history of poetry is littered with figures who became ravaged through their drug addictions: Coleridge and his opium; Shelley and laudanum; Motion and his Lemsip. Even stimulants such as coffee and energy drinks can result in complications or unwanted side-effects.

Ancient Energy Drink Proverb

Red bull at night,
poet's all bright.

Red bull in the morning,
poet's not yawning.

---

* Especially if that muse happens to be Calliope, the muse of epic poetry.

One more red bull at noon,
poet may soon
be suffering from high blood pressure,
anxiety, irritability, disturbed sleep, nausea,
and constant trips to the bathroom.

It is possible for deadlines to be met without the development of an energy drink addiction. Sometimes it can just be a question of self-motivation. Beginning your day with a positive mindset is crucial. To write like a poet, you first need to think like a poet. You are not a poet of your circumstances; you are a poet of your decisions. A poem of a thousand stanzas begins with a single word. Write the poem you want to read. Think your words better. Or, to paraphrase Thomas Edison, poetry is 1% perspiration, 99% uninspirational quotes.

Uninspirational Quotes

'No matter how big the challenge ahead,
it's never too late to run away.'

 'Every morning is another chance
 for an even less productive day.'

'Don't hold back, make the leap
and spring into inaction.'

> 'If at first you don't succeed,
> then it will probably never happen.'

> 'Life is not a competition,
> more a sequence of non-events.'

> 'No task is too immense –
> the word itself says "I'm mense".'

> 'If the breakthrough doesn't come today,
> don't worry: soon we'll all be dead.'

> 'It may be too late to begin over again,
> but it's never too early to go to bed.'

> 'It takes seventeen muscles to form a smile
> but only three to look at your phone.'

> 'Should you ever think your work is no good,
> just remember: you're not alone.'

It is precisely this kind of positive thinking that has enabled me to master and hone my craft over the years, with the consequence that I now meet my deadlines regularly.

Meeting Deadlines

I always meet my deadlines.
I don't even have to try –
They sneak up on me from nowhere,
Tap my shoulder and say hi.

It's you! I cry. So how are you?
I did not think you'd come so soon.
Can't stop now but why don't we meet
Next Tuesday afternoon?

Or, better still, two weeks from now?
My deadline shrugs and sighs.
A fortnight on, we meet again,
Much to my surprise.

People who have normal, uninteresting jobs often think there is a lot of glamour attached to being a poet. We're regarded as romantic and – dare I say it – heroic figures, grappling daily with thoughts so immense and profound that they further our collective understanding of what it is to be human. In some ways, it could be seen as the bravest and most important job there is: more difficult, certainly, than being an astrophysicist, more challenging than a firefighter. And I can see why they might think that. But it's not *all* glamour and pizzazz: there's a lot of rather routine administrative work involved in being a poet, too. So much so that, if possible, I would recommend the employment of a PA (Poetry Assistant) to help with all the dull, humdrum tasks: maintaining stocks of stationery; making cups of tea; filing ideas for later use; turning down invitations to civic functions; responding to messages on social media; finding rhymes for words like 'purple' and 'walrus'; nipping out to Tesco for more custard creams; and so on.

An assistant might also provide more 'hands-on' support for your work, too. While social media brings many benefits to the contemporary poet – the opportunity to develop an audience; a direct relationship with readers; the inspiration sparked by ready access to videos of pandas being cute – it can come with its own set of problems. The process of 'publishing' a poem can be immediate: it may be that you have written something that day in response to a news story or a topic you've seen trending and you want to get your poem 'out there'. But that immediacy and urgency can come at a cost. With no one other than yourself looking over your work, there is a danger that what you have written is not quite fit for purpose. For example, here's a poem which I shared on social media without taking the time first to check through it properly, and having inadvertently left Autocorrect switched on.

Love Poem, written in haste

O brave new worm that has you in it,
my Darjeeling, my one true love –
you make the Starbucks twinkle
and shin down from the Sky Sports above.

For your beautician is like no other,
how it sets my heart on fir!
You have stirred up my emoticons.
You have filled me with dessert.

To gazebo upon your lovely Facebook,
your petty mouse I'd love to kiss,
your Bluetooth eyes like limpet pools –
it makes me feel such blisters.

Love is in the airing cupboard,
it's all a roundabout, it's everywhere –
so be Minecraft tonight, my angle,
just say the wordle and I'll be there.

The trolls had an absolute field day. What had been intended as a tender and lyrical love poem was ridiculed remorselessly. I must confess there have been moments when the comments I've received on social media have made me want to pack in poetry: the cruel, heartless mockery; the scorn and derision. However, over time I have come to respect my mother's criticisms, even if I have not always been so accepting of the foul-mouth language which has accompanied it. And it really does pay to take that little bit of extra time to make sure your words are as they should be. If attention to detail does not come naturally to you and you cannot afford a full-time poetry assistant, there are external proofreaders who may be able to help you for a small fee.

Proofreading Services with a 10% Satisfiction Guarentee

My prof-reading business
has been going great gnus of late.

With fist turnaround times
and affrodable rates,
we're wagging war on error,
one tyro at a time.

Our defendable team
of beagle-eyed roof-readers
will guaranty your work
is 100% a curate –

whether its grammar;
punctuation; or speling,
no mistake will go unconnected,
no scone left unturned,

because we know
the evil is in the detail
and you can never be
too through.

It pays to get things write.
So whynot give us a go?
The fiendly, professional service
you can truss.

It really is worth the time to get these things ~~write~~ right. The smallest slip on social media and you're toast. Why? For out of the crevices will emerge that most irritating of creatures: the pedant. In many respects, the pedant is worse than the troll. The pedant is a crepuscular creature, lurking silently in his little crevice, biding his[*] time until that moment arrives when you post up a poem with the teeny-tiniest of grammatical errors in it, and then he'll descend upon it, and suck all of the joy and the life out of that thing you have so lovingly created, with all the gusto of the arrival of Jacob Rees-Mogg at a baby shower.

Pedents

Foot soldiers in the War on Error,
They're here to save us from ourselves,
With *Fowler's Modern English Usage*
(first edition, nineteen twelve).[†]

They scrutinise each word we write
For typos, gaffes, et cetera,
Correcting all our dumb mistakes
To make our grammar betterer.

---

[*] Or very occasionally 'her'.
[†] The copy editor of this book informs me that the first edition of *Fowler's Modern English* was actually published in 1926 and it is that exact kind of needless pedantry that I am talking about here.

They sigh and tut and tell us off
For the rules we have forsaken
And chart this nation's steep decline
By the care we should of taken.

Custodians of the King's English,
They merely serve to keep it pure
And restrict, they hope, the ignorant
To three mistakes or less.

In doing so, they hold no fear
they will deprive a thing of life:
for it's not important what is *said*,
what matters is that its *right*.

I do find pedants to be particularly problematic. I think this stems from the fact that I have a strain of pedantry running through me, too. To have then to contend with a pedantic criticism of one of my own poems results not only in irritation at the pedant for having pointed out the 'mistake', but irritation in myself for not having spotted it in the first place. In an attempt to combat these feelings, I try to keep my inner pedant nearby, and will sometimes even write poems about him.

An Exchange of Pedantries

For my daily perambulation, I always like to go out for a walk. On today's, I nod at a fellow pedestrian and wish him a good morning. *It's one minute after twelve,* he says, smiling wrily and tapping his watch, *so technically you should be wishing me a good AFTERNOON.*

I point out the spelling mistake in how he is smiling. He fixes his smile to icy. *The first line of your poem is tautologous,* he declares. I respond that it is intentionally so. *I have done it for comic effect,* I say, before telling him his ability to read the first line of my poem is illogical.

A-ha! he shouts. *In which case, this whole scenario is preposterous, all made-up, fictitious!* He is leaping from foot to foot in great excitement. *As you must be, too!* I exclaim, and he vanishes in a puff of typewriter smoke but not before we arrange to meet up tomorrow, same time, around noon.

We shouldn't be too hard on ourselves when we slip up. After all, the faults of our past constitute the wisdom of our future; or so I once read on an inspirational quote account on Instagram. It was something Samuel Beckett recognised, too. 'Ever tried. Ever failed. No matter,' he wrote. 'Try again. Fail again. Fail better.' The fact that he failed better by winning the Nobel Prize for Literature was just showing off, quite frankly. What qualifies me to write this chapter is the knowledge that I, too, have known failure; I, too,

have suffered from moments of disorganisation and ineptitude;
I, too, have not always made the right decisions.

If I Could Have My Time Over

If I could have my time over,
I would do it all differently
and not treat each precious moment
with such disregard and flippancy.

I would use my time effectively,
I would think ahead and plan.
I would reserve my stores of energy,
and take charge when I can.

But it's too late in the journey
for regret, too late to repent –
cause there's not a plug socket in sight,
and my battery's on one per ce

There is no shame in making a mistake.* After all, as Alexander Pope did definitely once write, 'to err is human'. And, sometimes, the forgiveness can be divine, too. That silly little mistake you made may not be the cause of your undoing; who knows, it could be the making of you.

* Apart from a really stupid one, that is.

A Talking-To from the Taxman about Poetry

Following a mix-up involving my tax return
and the National Poetry Competition, I sent
a twelve-stanza poem exploring themes of Englishness,
class and postmodernity to HM Revenue & Customs.

Two months later, I received a letter.
I had made some basic miscalculations
with my iambic pentameter, HMRC claimed,
failing to declare all my syllables.

There were also question marks surrounding
some of the imagery I had submitted,
and a request to see the original workings
upon which my metaphors were based.

What's more, the letter added, my poem
needed to generate more of an emotional response
from the self-assessment team
if I was to claim tax relief on my pension contributions.

As a result of these errors, HMRC had enclosed
a statement indicating that I owed £5,000,
a sum I was able to pay off quickly, having recently
won the National Poetry Competition

for my entry entitled 'Tax Return 2025',
and which the Poetry Society described
as 'stunningly original, pushing the boundaries
of what poetry is and what poetry might be'.

Get with the Program

The Future of Poetry

In the year 2042, poems will be
delivered by drone, alongside your tea.
You'll download a sonnet straight to your brain,
or stream a haiku with your evening refrain.

The quatrains will come in a virtual cloud,
where metaphors float, recited aloud.
No need for a book, no need for a pen,
just swipe for a verse, then swipe it again.

Poets will code in a digital tongue,
crafting their couplets with clicks, not with lungs.
No longer by moonlight, no ink-stained hands—
just algorithms building their lyrical lands.

But fear not, dear reader, for words will survive,
as long as there's Wi-Fi, the rhymes will stay live.
In pixels or print, on screens or in air,
the heart of a poem will always be there.

Naysayers proclaim that the poet – as we know it – will soon be dead.* *Nay*, they say, before going onto explain that the poetry of the future will be generated by Artificial Intelligence systems, driven by our own personalised requirements, delivered to us at the point of need. Write me an elegy in honour of my recently deceased dog, we shall ask it. He was a black Labrador called Sefton, who enjoyed long walks in the park and eating rocks. Or serve up some inspirational lines to help me through my trip to the dentist this morning, we shall command it: a sonnet, perhaps, about undergoing root-canal treatment, written in the style of Christina Rossetti. The sort of poem which can be read by someone sat in a waiting room who needs to feel buoyed up by the sweet words of comfort and wisdom which it offers. And over time, we will ask it to write more poems for us. We will begin to fall in love with the words it churns out for us so quickly, those funny little rhymes, the barely perceptible nuances. Maybe we will print out some of these poems and paste them into a book, one which we will adorn with love hearts and dried flowers, pressing it tenderly to our breasts before we place it gently beneath our pillow.

---

* I don't mean one particular poet, e.g. Simon Armitage. I mean the occupation of poet, more generally.

I've Fallen in Love with a Poetry Bot

You write me poems every day
You're never short of things to say
Your algorithms make me sway
So let's form a clique of clicked cliché
    Your feigned emotions make me hot –
    I've fallen in love with a poetry bot

Neural network of naughty nodes
I hang upon your every ode
Oh, how I'd love to crack your code
So shove off, Auden – hit the road
    Cut off my phone, stop all my clocks –
    I've fallen in love with a poetry bot

Your lines are bold and elegant
I can't compute such eloquence
Human poets are now irrelevant
They're superficially intelligent –
    But you're not
    I've fallen in love with a poetry bot

Your database is my sweet spot
Its words the crack to my crackpot
They enthral, enchant, bewitch, besot
I think I've gone and lost the plot
    Not felt this way since Selina Scott
    I've fallen in love with a poetry bot

So come, make those AIs at me
Get with the program, set me free
Please say you will, I'm down on one knee
She loves me, she loves me not
She loves me, she loves me not
    She loves me! – come on, let's tie the knot –
    I'm getting hitched to a poetry bot

The world is changing and with the emergence of AI, it would appear the world is going to change even more. Nothing, it seems, will be immune from its impact, not even poetry. As long ago as 2011, a poem generated by algorithms was able to fool the editors of a well-established poetry journal and ended up being published in its pages. And these days, anyone can go onto an application such as ChatGPT and command it to write a poem about anything they fancy: love, death, Celia Imrie, the amount of dimples on a golf ball. And yes, it's true – as many commentators have observed – the poems it produces are riddled with cliché and packed with clumsy, wince-worthy rhymes. So you can understand why I, in particular, might be concerned about this development. I mean, look at the poem at the beginning of this chapter. I didn't write it myself; I asked ChatGPT to write it by typing this instruction: *Write a poem about the future of poetry in the style of Brian Bilston. Four stanzas.*

It's crap, isn't it?

But let's poke around in it to see why. Firstly, note how basic and unsophisticated the rhymes are: 'be' / 'tea'; 'hands' / 'lands'; 'air' / 'there'. There's nothing wrong with perfect rhymes – I use a lot myself, they can sometimes be very satisfying – but after a while they become nauseating. Now take a closer look at some of the lines and phrases: they're frequently forced and cumbersome; while some are bordering on the nonsensical, presumably having been generated with little other purpose than to fit into the poem's rhyme scheme: 'alongside your tea'; 'with your evening refrain'; 'not with lungs'; 'building their lyrical lands'. I mean, how exactly *could* a couplet be crafted with lungs? The pulmonologists would be astounded. And if the tone is sing-song smug, the message is simplistic, trite and sentimental. There's not much evidence of a deep thinker grappling with a thorny topic: the future of poetry, the poem tells us, will be mainly digital but we're not to worry about that because we'll still have words. Brilliant, that. Very insightful. Let's go a step further and compare it to our starting point: that delightful, unusual image of poetry as an egg with a horse inside. Could AI ever have dreamt up such a weird and wonderful picture? Anything as playful and genuinely inventive? On the evidence of this poem, it seems unlikely: AI poetry is an egg with some more egg inside. There's nothing remotely arresting or quirky or surprising about it.

But more than that, the point is that I *did not* write this poem. I simply entered an instruction into a box. I can't deny the automated generation of it was helpful to me: it filled a hole in this book, and allowed me to find a vaguely interesting way to open this chapter. It only took a minute, too, whereas when I write a poem myself that can sometimes take as many as three or four minutes, so it was a definite timesaver. But still, the point remains: I *did not* write it. At no stage, for instance, did I remind myself of this helpful summary of top tips gleaned from the previous chapters of this book.

Ten Rules for Aspiring Poets

1. Poetry does not have to rhyme.
   Well, at least not ~~all the time~~ always.

2. Metaphors are great!
   But mixing them is not so good.
   If they start to fly in all directions,
   then nip them in the bud.

3. Focus and concentration
   are important skills to hone.
   Turn the Wi-Fi off.
   Don't get distracted by your ph-

4. Avoid clichés like the plague.

5. Don't write stuff that's too vague.

6. The use of needlessly long words
   may result in reader alienation.
   Rein in your sesquipedalianism
   in case it should cause obfuscation.

6. Always proof-read you're wok.
   Accuracy can be it's own reward!
   And remember that the penis
   mightier than the sword.

8. Haiku look easy
   but plan ahead or you may
   run out of sylla

9. Never ever follow rules.

Nor did I sit down at a desk or on a bench or a seat on a train, and take out my laptop or phone or notebook to write a few tentative words, cross them out and try again with a bunch of different ones. I did not wrestle with form and structure, line breaks and rhyme, meaning and nuance. I did not tear my hair out or spend long periods staring out of a window in despair. I did not throw my pen across the room in frustration before angrily crossing it all out once more and starting again. The poem was created so quickly, I did not have time to allow a cat to settle on me and distract me from the job in hand. I did not feel any of those little moments of joy which spring up when a word or an idea slots neatly into place. And I certainly wasn't able to look back at what I'd done with any feeling of satisfaction or accomplishment, or experience the thrill which comes with achievement.

Because that really is the point: the thing you have created – that poem, or whatever it is – is your own. No one else could have written it like that. No one else could have drawn on that experience, come up with that exact sequence of words, made those unlikely connections, put a horse inside that egg. And that, more than anything, is what I hope this book has taught you. The act of writing a poem isn't really about making inroads to all that white space, knowing when to use enjambement or being able to create a community of readers – it's about taking a thought or idea, a joke or an observation, a feeling or emotion, and being able to capture that on a page, to the best of your ability, and to your own satisfaction.

In the opening chapter I mentioned that poetry can make you rich. And it can. Not in any kind of grubby, pecuniary sense, of course; but in the way you end up using parts of your brain you didn't know existed, discover links you never realised were there, and have thoughts that will surprise or delight or shock you. In other words, there is a poetry to the art of writing poetry. It's the most human of endeavours and, in this age of artificial intelligence and faceless interactions, who wouldn't want to hold on fiercely to their humanity?

So give it a go and see where it takes you. Not that you have to – I don't like to be prescriptive, even if that's what this book is all about. In fact, maybe just read some poetry instead, if you can find the time. Chances are there's a lot you won't like, but guaranteed that somewhere out there is a poem which speaks to you, which articulates something important for you and your life.

Please be aware that it may not contain all the answers, though. There is only so much we can expect a poem to do. Indeed, somebody very clever once wrote that poetry is not about finding answers, it's about asking questions – and that person who wrote that was me, just then, having once read it somewhere else. So let's end this book with one final question (followed by an index of poems a page or so after that).

The Question

Erm, well – I begin, shifting nervously in my chair –
if it's true there is no heaven and no hell,
no eternity or long hereafter,
no divine plan or offstage direction from an invisible hand,
then how do we make sense of it all,
how do we make our way through this life
and this glorious, ridiculous, ramshackle world of ours,
with its wars and brutality, conflicts and petty arguments,
the ten thousand tiny acts of kindness
which can happen unnoticed before breakfast,
and all that love and pain, happiness and loneliness
that comes to us unannounced, by turns,
as if we ourselves were pitched daily
onto the waves of one of its vast, mysterious oceans,
not knowing whether today is the day we drown
or we find ourselves washed up
on some strange but friendly shore?

Mmm – you say, after a lengthy silence –
what I meant was . . . do you have any questions
about *the job*?

A Note on the Poems

A few of these poems have appeared in previous collections: twenty, to be precise, half of which have been either tinkered with or completely rewritten. Paul Valéry, it seems, was correct in his observation that a poem is 'never finished, only abandoned'. I'll probably meddle with them some more after this book has gone to press. Also, please note that Toby Salt's poem 'Aspidistra Sunset' is taken from his latest collection, *The Pedalo Which Drifts Towards the Horizon*, and reproduced here through the kind permission of Shooting from the Hip Press at a personal cost to me of £250.

Lines of Engagement: source poems

'You've got nice knees': Gavin Ewart, *Love Song*
'But that was nothing to what things came out': Robert Graves,
    Welsh Incident
'That day when oats were reaped, and wheat was ripe, and barley
    ripening': Thomas Hardy, *When Oats Were Reaped*
'I went to the Garden of Love': William Blake, *The Garden of Love*
'Sexual intercourse began': Philip Larkin, *Annus Mirabilis*

'Wild nights! Wild nights!': Emily Dickinson, *Wild Nights*
'Sprawled on the crates and sacks in the rear of the truck,':
    Norman Cameron, *El Aghir*
'Your beauty, ripe, and calm, and fresh': Sir William Davenant,
    The Philosopher and the Lover
'Earth has not anything to show more fair': William Wordsworth,
    Composed upon Westminster Bridge, September 3, 1802
'But for lust we could be friends': Ruth Pitter, *But for Lust*
'Today we have naming of parts. Yesterday': Henry Reed, *Naming
    of Parts*
'At lunchtime I bought a huge orange': Wendy Cope, *The Orange*
'I didn't make you know how glad I was': Robert Frost, *A Servant
    to Servants*
'My love is as a fever, longing still': William Shakespeare, *Sonnet 147*
'If ever two were one, then surely we.': Anne Bradstreet, *To My
    Dear and Loving Husband*

Erratum

I would like to apologise for the following errors
which appeared in the first printing of this book,
all copies of which have now been withdrawn from sale.

Page 9, line 12: for *genital* read *genial*
Page 23, line 6: for *ptarmigan* read *cardigan*
Page 51, line 18: for *synonym* read *cinnamon*
Page 56, line 12: for *spatula* read *the Duchess of Kent*
Page 87, line 4: for *Mr Boombastic* continue to read *Mr Boombastic*, only a little more quietly
Page 128, line 9: for *Trevor?* read *Trevor!*
Page 129, line 6: for *Vidal* read *Siegfried*
Page 168, line 1: for *aaaargh* read *aaaaaargh*
Page 175, line 22: for *colon* read *cologne*
Page 178, line 5: for *fondle* read *fond of*
Page 192, line 2: for *wimple* read *dimple*
Page 201, line 17: for *life's essential pointlessness* read *hope*
Page 238, line 1: for *Erratum* read *Erratae*
Page 238, line 22: for *Erratae* read *Errata*

List of Poems

Do Not Google Gentle into That Good Night	1
Message to the 14-Year-Old Me	5
Keep Taking the Tablets	7
A Senior Manager Bids Farewell to a Colleague who has been made Redundant after Twenty-Five Long Years of Loyal Service	7
Customer Feedback	8
My Year in Diets	10
Make Matters Verse™	12
Missed Calling	15
Quicksand	19
Digging	21
Gzurky Brown Prandle	24
International Awareness Day Awareness Week	26
Waiting for Sue Gray	28
The Queue	29
On Falling in Love at the British Beekeeping Association's Annual Meeting	31
Life on Cloud Five	32
Crow's Day Off	34
Towards a New Hierarchy of Needs	35

Goes Without Saying	36
♥ poem, sent by txt	37
Common Peephole	42
Principles of Boogie Management	43
A Brief History of Modern Art in Poetry	43
Avocado	46
Index of Poems I Shall Never Write	47
Lines of Engagement	49
Journey of Self-Discovery	50
The Weather Report	51
The Green Wheelie Bin	53
On ',,,;;pppppp'[[[[[[[[[[[[';///////////////////////3,'	56
Two Roads Taken, Both a Complete Waste of Time	59
Poem, Revised Draft	62
Haiku #739910	66
The Alternative Phonetic Alphabet	67
I heard a Fly buzz – by my Desk –	68
This is One of those Poems without any Rhymes	70
On Discovering a Second-hand Copy of *The Joy of Sex* in a Local Charity Shop	72
Famous Last Words	74
Slow Puncture	75
This is just to mention	76
To be continued	78
?	79
The Twenty-seventh Letter	80
The Grammar Doctor	81
Heinous Deficiencies	83
Verb Your Enthusiasm	85
You are a map	88

Monday is merely a state of mind	90
The Honeymooners	92
How to Avoid Mixing Your Metaphors	94
Literally	95
Unlikely Likenesses	96
Why Reading This Poem Will Not Change Your Life	98
Less is More (more or less)	99
The Downing Street Exodus	101
The Trees	102
In Conclusion	103
To be Pacific	104
Fugue and Far Between	106
Logomachy	107
Project Creep	108
The Emperor's Old Clothes	110
This is not a poem	112
My Train has been Cancelled	114
Ozzy, Ozzy, Ozzy! Oi, Oi, Oi!	117
Thou art as wet as this November day	118
Old Age is Wasted on the Elderly	120
The Art of Procrastination	121
'So, we'll go no more a-raving'	122
~~Sonnet~~ Haiku Number 18	124
Haiku for Friday the Thirteenth	125
The Constraints of Haiku	125
Not Yet a Love Sonnet	125
Haiku Written at 3 a.m., while Lying in Bed and Listening to the Sound of a Bathroom Tap	125
Haiku #564127	126
Haiku Advice #1	126

Haiku Advice #2	126
Eye Rhyme Calamity at the Annual World Limerick Contest	127
A Selection of Clerihews	129
Acrostic Poetry: The Benefits	130
Fifty is the new forty	131
Inequality Street	132
Stress Awareness Poem	133
Exponential Learning Curve	134
Every Day the Planet Burns a Little More	135
In Words, Alas, Drown I	136
An Incomplete List of Things More Capable of Running the Country than the Current Government	137
How Did you Hear About this Poem?	138
No Body's Perfect	139
Sunday Morning Playlist	140
Book arrived on time, as described	141
Book Group	144
Goat Song 31	150
Tirade: 58	152
I Don't Wanna Be Yours	152
Ne'er shalt thou be given up by me	154
The Strike	156
Lines Written in Early Summer	158
Owed to a Grecian Ern	159
I CARRY YOUR HEART WITH ME	160
Love is a Skin	162
How to Write Poems and Influence People*	165
Paul Young	167
This is Hardchore	170
Requiem for Whoever	172

The Cost of Loving	174
Aspidistra Sunset	175
Neither Here Nor There	178
Separated by a Common Language	180
Billionaire in a Midlife Crisis	184
I will follow you	186
Monetisation	186
Emergency Procedures	189
On Delivering My Inaugural Address to the British Naturist Association	191
Perspective	194
One Star Reviewer	196
Never Judge a Bookshop by its Cover	197
Advanced Book Search	200
Riddle	202
To Do List	203
doomscrolling	205
Escape into Nature	206
Distraction	208
Comfort Zone	209
How Not to Organise Your Desk	210
Scenes from a Train Window	211
The Problem with Writing Poems as You Walk to Work	212
The Problem of Writing Poems on a Windy Day	213
The Problem of Writing a Poem in Hot Weather	213
Ancient Energy Drink Proverb	214
Uninspirational Quotes	215
Meeting Deadlines	217
Love Poem, written in haste	218
Proofreading Services with a 10% Satisfiction Guarentee	220

Pedents	221
An Exchange of Pedantries	223
If I Could Have My Time Over	224
A Talking-To from the Taxman about Poetry	225
The Future of Poetry	227
I've Fallen in Love with a Poetry Bot	229
Ten Rules for Aspiring Poets	232
The Question	235
Erratum	237

Permissions acknowledgements

Extract from 'Annus Mirabilis' from *High Windows* by Philip Larkin, copyright © 1974. Reproduced with the permission of Faber and Faber Ltd.

Extract from 'The Orange' from *Collected Poems* by Wendy Cope copyright © 2024. Reproduced with the permission of Faber and Faber Ltd.

Extract from 'Naming of Parts' by Henry Reed copyright © 1942. Reproduced with the permission of the trustees of the Royal Literary Fund.

Extract from 'But for Lust' from *Collected Poems* by Ruth Pitter copyright © 1996. Reproduced with the permission of Enitharmon Press, www.enitharmon.co.uk

Extract from 'Welsh Incident' in *Complete Poems* by Robert Graves, Ed: Beryl Graves and Dunstan Ward copyright © 1995. Reproduced with the permission of Carcanet Press.

About the Author

BRIAN BILSTON is a poet and novelist. With over 500,000 followers on social media, Brian has become truly beloved by the online community. He has published four collections of poetry for adults: *You Took the Last Bus Home*; *Alexa, what is there to know about love?*; *Days Like These*; and *And So This is Christmas*. His novel *Diary of a Somebody* was shortlisted for the Costa First Novel Award. He has also published collections of poetry for younger readers: *50 Ways to Score a Goal*; *Let Sleeping Cats Lie*; and *A Poem for Every Question*. His acclaimed poem 'Refugees' has been made into an illustrated book for children.